American Bistro

Irena Chalmers an

An Irena Chalmers Book

CONTEMPORARY
BOOKS, INC.
CHICAGO ■ NEW YORK

NOTE TO THE READER:

This is a new kind of cookbook, as you will see the moment you look at its Contents.

American cooking today is a celebration of diversity, of pleasure in combining exquisite elements in new ways, of the friendly sharing of ideas. In words and pictures, I have tried to create an *impression* of what I perceive is happening to food all over this country, from the grandest restaurants to the bistros to the diners. So I have deliberately intermingled the chefs and restaurants and the glorious foods among the recipes to convey some of the incredibly rich variety of ingredients, settings and methods of presentation, and to give you the feeling of excitement and sharing I discern, where each is inspired by the quality of the other.

It is a personal sampling of the best new recipes I could find, adapted for entertaining at home and illuminated with perfectly gorgeous color photographs. I like to call this heady blending of different foodstuffs, styles of cooking and ideas *American Bistro*—and I hope you enjoy it.

IRENA CHALMERS

Staff for American Bistro

MANAGING EDITOR: Jean Atcheson
EDITOR: Barbara Spiegel
ART DIRECTOR: Barbara Asch
PICTURE EDITORS: Laurie Winfrey, Lyssa Papazian
COVER DESIGNER: Mary Ann Joulwan
RECIPE TESTERS: Jim Fobel, Mindy Heiferling, Michael Krondl,
    Lori Longbotham, Elizabeth Schneider, Elizabeth Wheeler
CONTRIBUTORS: Richard Atcheson, Robert Ostermann, Rebecca Trahan,
    Mary Backstrom

On the title page: Jonathan Waxman, one of the leaders in the new American cooking on both coasts, works with his staff in JAMS' kitchen in New York.

Contents page: Anne Rosenzweig, who both owns and cooks brilliantly in New York's Arcadia.

It was Phillip Cooke and Daniel Maye whose Fourth Symposium on American Cuisine provided me with the opportunity to talk to many of the remarkable chefs who are changing the way we are eating in America. I was already at work on this book, and their enthusiasm and support were most encouraging.

So let us now give praise to all the chefs and restaurant owners whom we harangued ceaselessly to coax from them their favorite recipes. For their patience, good humor and willingness to send menus, recipes and photographs back and forth with lightning speed, we are hugely grateful—and so is Federal Express.

I especially want to thank Bill Liederman, President of The New York Restaurant School, who graciously gave us permission to use the photograph of his splendidly futuristic Dine-O-Mat Restaurant—alas, now closed—on the cover of this book, and Ira Grandberg, who so generously shared with us his ideas about the architecture and design of good restaurants.

A special chortle of thanks to George Lang, whose personal Recipe for an American Bistro cost him half a night's sleep to write, but will surely take its place as yet another brilliantly witty original from one of the country's most original restaurateurs. For so many of us, his Café des Artistes is our favorite neighborhood restaurant, even though we may live in a neighborhood a thousand miles from New York.

And my gratitude, too, to Joseph Baum, who shared with us his eternal love affair with restaurants and who, in creating Aurora, has set new standards of excellence in the food we eat and the joyful settings in which we choose to eat it.

—IRENA CHALMERS

Table of Contents

A Sure-Fire Recipe
for an American Bistro

Yield:
One
Good-Sized
Bistro

HE COOKING UTENSILS:
About 4,000 square feet of space near a paved road.
1 very long lease, which is like the girdle on a fat lady:
maybe it's tight but it still lets her breathe.

INGREDIENTS

For the Dough:

Several sackfuls of money, preferably not yours and without
    strings attached

For Flavoring:

1 well-seasoned chef, male or female (between 120 and 200 pounds),
    preferably one whose ego has to be fed only once a day
1 bouquet garni of assorted cooks and key personnel. Average age
    should be 30 years old with a minimum of 20 years of experience
1 head bartender with 4 hands and no pockets
A medium-sized, all-purpose kitchen planner

Yeast:

1 fully grown manager who will make the BISTRO rise without
    too much kneading

Making the Sauce:

1 fully ripened interior designer (do not remove backbone)
1 fine-grained graphic designer and 1 uniform designer (optional)

Additional Ingredients:

5 billion kilowatts of energy combined with the firmness of Bo Derek
The combined leadership qualities of de Gaulle and Genghis Khan
The optimism of a person who is getting married for the 7th time
1,000 gallons of tact and resourcefulness (or more as needed)
A sprinkling of well-sifted originality

For the Topping:

1 public relations person, whipped until a froth has formed

Café des Artistes: bustling, cheerful and romantic, a landmark restaurant where the menu and wine list are constantly changed and improved by its owner, George Lang, a true Renaissance man— writer, violinist and passionate perfectionist.

METHOD

Before combining ingredients:

Conduct market study to match the taste of your market and the planned restaurant with your location, considering dozens of changeable and unchangeable conditions. After completing it, read it carefully and go with your instincts.

Step 1: Consider the total interlocking picture before beginning the cooking process.

Step 2: Mixing the Dough: You must control budget and scheduling, otherwise you'll end up with a disaster.

Step 3: You must define each segment of the preparation and cooking process; then divide it into individual tasks, giving them out to different specialists, and at the end—if you did your job properly—the recipe will add up to a living Bistro.

Step 4: You must be sure to train everybody as a true professional, remembering at all times that the American Bistro is a democratic and egalitarian institution where everyone should be treated with equal hospitality.

Step 5: What was called *Art de Cuisine* in the near past must be transformed into Good Food with a point of view served to a non-captive audience within a dining (not eating) ambiance.

Step 6: Serving Directions:

* In order to lower the failure factor you must consider the American Bistro as a social institution, a place for recreation and entertainment.

* You must learn how to produce quality in the age of shortcuts, serving food which is not of the blow-dried variety.

* This recipe will be considered a success by others as well if the Bistro offers flavor, freshness and friendliness and contributes happily towards the guests' hedonism.

NOTE: If you have carefully followed the above steps, you are ready to cast your jalapeño-cornbread upon the waters and let the good times roll . . . .

GEORGE LANG

Introduction

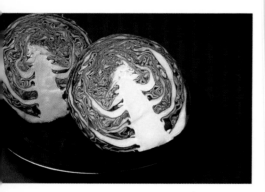

merica has long had its own distinctive style in music, films, art and architecture, but it is only very recently that we have developed our own unique style of cooking. It is both intriguing and fascinating to see how rapidly this New American Cooking has captured the imagination of the nation. It has been embraced enthusiastically from San Francisco to Seattle and from the Midwest to the North and East and the South.

Everywhere, we are flocking to the new restaurants, daring to savor new tastes, marveling at the dazzling decor and new freedom of choices when we dine out. Gone are the stuffy French restaurants, the beef Stroganoff, the rolling silver carts of steamed "roasts," the iceberg lettuce, canned string beans, satin dresses and corsages. Vanished, too, are the haughtily superior waiters whose self-appointed task seemed to be more to intimidate than to inform. In their place have come the chic new restaurants, charming bistros and comfortable neighborhood cafés, populated by young waitpersons, wearing cheerful smiles and sneakers, with snowy white aprons tied flatly around slim waists.

The pendulum is still swinging between the sumptuous and the sublime, the stark and the austere, and these contrasts of style are found not only in the restaurants but also in the food itself. In some places styles overlap, while at others they are more clearly defined. The revolution in the ways we are eating today is still evolving, and it is a wondrously intriguing game to try to sample it all and all at once. There are instant gratifications of new pleasures and old indulgences. We are seeing everything on the same menu—from sautéed breast of duck with fresh foie gras and cornmeal pancakes with caviar to Southern fried chicken, mashed potatoes and gravy.

Four years ago at the First Symposium on American Cuisine, innumerable hours were spent trying to define this so-called new cooking. By now we can freely admit that even if we do not know exactly how to establish a fence and boundaries around this emerging phenomenon, at least we can recognize it when we see it. Lydia Shire, the chef of Seasons restaurant in Boston, has said that trying to define American Cuisine is a lot like trying to pet a porcupine—there is no easy way to do it. And in fact there is much to be said for leaving the entire concept of the New American Cuisine and American Bistro ill defined, so that everyone can have the freedom to interpret it any way they wish!

Our interpretation of "Bistro" here is very broad and excludes none. It embraces all those new restaurants dedicated, each in its own way, but each one unstintingly, to excellence—in the ingredients, the cooking, the service, and the welcoming "feel" of the restaurant itself, which keeps loyal customers coming back again and again. These are places where a leisurely romance can flourish or business friends can talk without a sense of needing to pay a real-estate tax for renting the table for too long, places where a bunch of kids can feel at home or when a family comes to celebrate a birthday all will have agreed that this is a great place to have chosen.

Some of the new bistros are light, cheerful places with snowy white tablecloths spread on chunky tables. There are chunky glasses, chunky cutlery, big chunky white plates and big fans to stir the air-conditioned air. Often there are huge palm trees, and fresh garden flowers are always on display. Some are decorated with wildly eclectic furnishings, heightened by dazzlingly brilliant colors with lightning splashes of neon, reverberating with brain-hammering noise and crashing movement. Yet others are more restrained, recapturing the hushed atmosphere and soft, subtle elegance that have traditionally marked establishments that serve fine food.

Yet all these new places share many of the same attitudes to the food and the guests that they serve.

The whole bistro idea is as a very old one. It is perhaps best typified by a bustling, noisy restaurant in Paris called La Coupole. This brasserie-bistro is both a comfortable neighborhood restaurant and a landmark

Some still-lifes from the palette of the American Bistro—are they art or are they for eating? Or are they simply the freshest, biggest, most beautiful comestibles you ever dreamed might one day be put on *your* plate, too?

dining place, open from early in the morning until a closing time that is delayed until the very last sleepy, late-night revelers wander happily off in the wee small hours. You can go to La Coupole for lunch or dinner or a snack or a croissant whenever you wish, and dressed in formal evening clothes, a business suit or workman's overalls. No one ever tires of it because it becomes to the regulars as familiar as home; the foundation of the menu is always the same, yet there are always the surprises of the special dishes new each day. People go there to have a grand five-course dinner with five fine wines, but they are equally welcome if they drop in for a dozen winkingly fresh Belon oysters, just plucked from the icy salt water, and a glass of crisp cold Chablis at 2 A.M.

This was the kind of restaurant Jeremiah Tower had in mind when he opened his place, Stars, in San Francisco a year or two ago. He designed a menu so that his guests could come in and spend a long evening lingering over a very special meal, or with equal ease swallow a fast little seviche at the modest cost of $2.00, or a small individual pizza topped with smoked salmon for $3.00.

This is what the restaurants in the Eighties are all about . . . .

We have taken a look at many of the new restaurants across the country, some quite awesomely grand and some just the reverse, and found that they have many things in common. There is a passionate concern, almost an obsession, to eat fresh, pure ingredients at their peak of perfection. Indeed, the ideal is to arrange for the corn to be plucked and dropped into the already-boiling pot of water, at the same second the trout leaps from the lake and falls gasping onto the mesquite grill!

Short of this utopia, some, like Vernon and Charlene Rollins at the New Boonville Hotel in Mendocino, grow their own herbs, fruits and vegetables, and other chefs everywhere are contracting with local farmers to buy only the best of the best. To aid and abet this passion for newly plucked peaches, fresh crawfish, live lobsters and sweet violets, an incredible range of more exotic ingredients is being air-lifted from tiny hamlets to bustling cities. We are seeing an ever-increasing use of delicate basil, cilantro and other fresh herbs and audaciously bold, hot spices to flavor the favorite ingredients of the New American Cuisine: the piquant goat cheeses (now being made in at least 10 states), the brilliant black and yellow, as well as the more traditional green and red peppers and chilis,

The first bistros are said to have sprung up when the Allied armies occupied Paris after Napoleon's defeat at Waterloo, as simple, neighborhood cafés offering food and drink inexpensively to hungry diners. The word comes from the Russian for "be quick"—which was already a quality much admired. At left, a thoroughly modern bistro, Stars in San Francisco.

the New York fresh foie gras and California caviar, the smoked salmon, smoked tuna, smoked shrimp and smoked almost everything else, the duck breasts and quail and range-fed chickens, the caramelized onions and pecans, the red cabbage and crimson curled radicchio . . . .

We are eating a dozen varieties of oysters, along with sea scallops and farm-raised mussels, crawfish and catfish. We are joyfully devouring rabbits and lentils and pork and lamb sausage and black beans and molasses. Restaurants like Mustards in the Napa Valley are making their own condiments and ketchups and serving figs so fresh and so filled with sunshine that the memory of them will haunt many a snowy night.

We are no longer roasting and deep-fat frying, but grilling and stir-frying and steaming and wrapping our food in parchment and innovating dishes. We are all eating Paul Prudhomme's blackened redfish, along with lusty, crusty bread and sweet butter, and vegetables so tiny that they seem more appropriate for Tom Thumb than the Jolly Green Giant.

We are, most of all, having a glorious time, sharing in the abundance of the good earth, shouting applause and encouragement for the chefs, and spurring them on to new creations to delight us. Meanwhile, they are like a jam of jazz musicians, playing set after set, variation after variation, spurring each other on with flair and imagination until we are presented with one of those awesome creations—like five different kinds of smoked salmon reclining in four different rippling rivers of sauces, topped by three different kinds of caviar and counterpointed by a lone crawfish pirouetting on a single sublime pea.

The recipes that follow are those that I have enjoyed eating at many of these restaurants, and have chosen for us to cook at home. I think they are among the best currently available and I hope they will nourish you and your friends on many happy evenings. I hope to have left out as many restaurants as I have included, for in this way we can keep adding more to our growing repertoire and our menus will be constantly refreshed and renewed with the anticipation of more, and yet more.

Food As Theater

In the American Bistro, all the world's a stage and, if you dine there, you're on it and right in the dazzling center. So, of course, is everybody else. And nobody upstages the food.

A table for two was never like this before—with every element placed in perfect balance. In the best of these new cafés and restaurants, a kind of apotheosis of ambiance is achieved, a new heaven of designer tiles and tables and chairs, china and glassware, lighting and linen. On one plate, one perfect bunch of miniature grapes, a perfect breast of duck, a spot of sauce; on the other, a perfect hamburger. Delivering this, one perfect waitperson.

How to incorporate this? How to rise to the challenge of such *luxe?* The answer is simple. Dress well, pick a perfect companion, and bring along lots of perfect money.

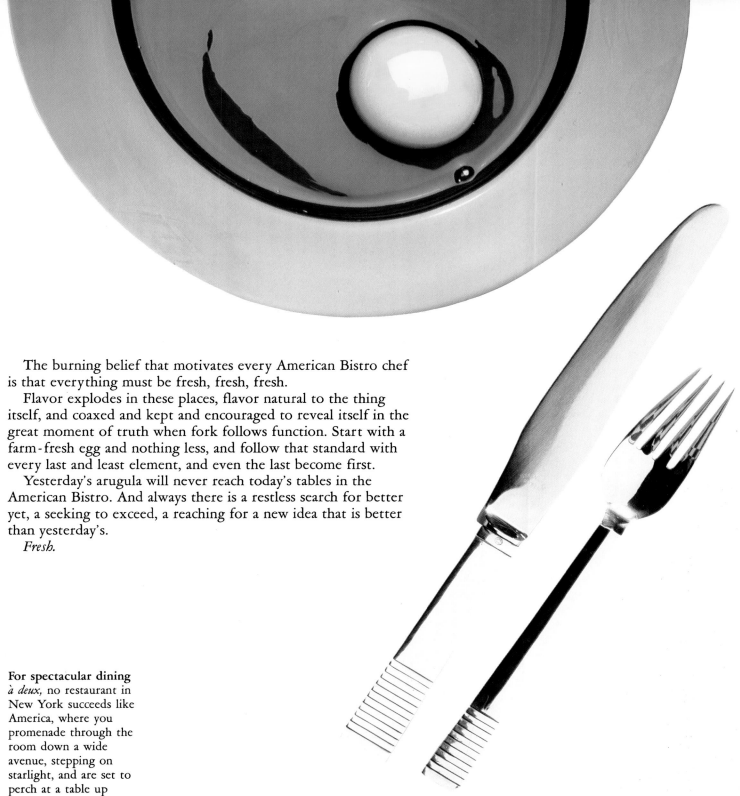

The burning belief that motivates every American Bistro chef is that everything must be fresh, fresh, fresh.

Flavor explodes in these places, flavor natural to the thing itself, and coaxed and kept and encouraged to reveal itself in the great moment of truth when fork follows function. Start with a farm-fresh egg and nothing less, and follow that standard with every last and least element, and even the last become first.

Yesterday's arugula will never reach today's tables in the American Bistro. And always there is a restless search for better yet, a seeking to exceed, a reaching for a new idea that is better than yesterday's.

Fresh.

For spectacular dining *à deux,* no restaurant in New York succeeds like America, where you promenade through the room down a wide avenue, stepping on starlight, and are set to perch at a table up above the mere, the better for *them* to see *you.* The murals create a montage of the prototypical symbols of America: Miss Liberty, an eagle, a streamliner, and you.

Setting Scenes

The design is integral, but it should never fight the food for first place.

hat is essential to a restaurant's success is what we, as patrons, are not particularly intended to notice: the set itself. There is here a grand design that penetrates far deeper than the mirrors facing mirrors facing mirrors, the broad avenue through a forest of pedestal tables, the twinkling stairway to Paradise. There is here a coherent, but invisible scheme.

You should enter a restaurant new to you in the expectation of being enthralled—and, if the place works, you will be. Indeed, you may wonder how in the world something so perfectly apt can have happened to you in a public place. Could a spell have been cast upon you? You're right; it has.

The American Bistro is no accident, flung there by a set of hulking deliverpeople. Nor did some effervescent person with a star-tipped wand sprinkle fairy dust upon the threshold where you stand. The magic—and it *is* a kind of magic—was all concocted for you in the architect's plan.

With restaurants as with anything else, architects work with the space available. Sometimes they have the opportunity to build a new structure; more commonly, especially in large cities, they take charge of existing spaces and interpret them anew. In whatever case, they are our psychologists of the environment, and we are in their hands more than we may know. Our moods are thoroughly tinkered with in their every elevation—and never more so than when we go out to dine. A well-planned environment, like a good wine, can measurably increase our sense of well-being, even of affluence; but we are not supposed to notice that the architects have been at work.

"I don't want people coming into one of my restaurants to think 'an architect designed this,' " says Ira Grandberg, a young New York architect who has made a specialty of restaurant design. (His works include the Dine-O-Mat, the interior of which is pictured on our cover, and the Acute Café, shown on the previous pages.) "Basically," he says, "the design must never fight the food for first place."

So Grandberg's intent, like that of all the architects who work in this field, is to make the work as unobtrusive as possible, in a manipulation so deft that you never realize what is happening to you.

"Ideally," says Grandberg, "I like to design a restaurant so that you can recognize your seating options the moment you walk in the door—as if you were presented with a perfectly prepared plate of food and were deciding in which order to attack its elements."

To give people options which they can control, he organizes restaurant space into zones. Like all restaurant architects, he has to work with a room that will be filled with tables and chairs, but he insists that the environment must come first—an environment in which the tables and seating form an integral part. "I try to work within an architectural envelope that has an inherent organization," he says, "so that people can be subliminally aware of it. You want to have a sense of visual alternatives, even though you are not aware of the banquettes functioning as low partitions, or a variation in ceiling heights or lights, the architectural

Previous page: The quiet coloring of the Acute Café, in New York City, offers a backdrop against which each day's diners provide a constantly shifting show. At lower right, even the chefs get into the act at New York's American Harvest, arranging the portions just so; far right, it's lunchtime again at Primavera in Minneapolis; above, hot peppers are tops in the American Bistro.

directors of space that are influencing you. I want people to be comfortable without knowing why they feel that way."

To achieve this, an architect has to work in two scales: what Grandberg calls the macro scale of initial awareness, which is all-enveloping, and the micro scale of the individual table, set and ceiling—the inner envelope. From that subtle sense of security, he feels, one should be able to look out and see the other diners framed in a structured way. "We should never feel overpowered by those who are sharing a meal with us," he says.

Talking with an architect like Ira Grandberg, it begins to make sense that we can feel so much at ease in so many quite different kinds of places. The magic of the American Bistro setting, it seems, originates on an architect's drafting table—the fruit of years of study and observation and trial and error, and a high degree of creative glee.

And in all these settings the food will be the star. It is, after all, the main point of the entire exercise, and its colors must shine forth without competition. Thus, in the American Bistro, the color of the walls is liable to be buff, beige, pale rose—a neutral field against which both the food and those who feast on it can stand out in bold relief. We, meanwhile, are the supporting players, and our movement within the envelope provides the texture and animation that bring the set to life. Every night it's a new show, and the best thing is that we're all invited.

A New Dawn

*Turning
the lights
back on,*

oseph Baum, one of the premier restaurant-makers in America today, has brought innovations and flourishes of every sort to the evolution of the American Bistro in our time, in the creation of what he has called "eating and drinking entertainments."

In this work, one supreme obsession has dominated his thinking: light. As a consequence, Joe Baum must be credited with having turned the lights back on in restaurants all over this country, after years and years of imitative Continental gloom.

Baum didn't just turn on the lights. He threw back the curtains and let in the day, in restaurant after restaurant under his control. Consider the litany of his works:

THE FOUR SEASONS—airy space and height to spare, everywhere, suffused in the light of spring or fall or whatever season of the year is outside, brought inside through a shimmering, constantly rippling mass of metal chains.

LA FONDA DEL SOL—literally, The House of the Sun, and light-years ahead of its time, with an entrance emblazoned with a glittering sun and a 40-foot-long broiling wall, long before the mesquite craze. The first major restaurant in the United States to treat south-of-the-border food seriously, La Fonda vibrated with the colors of the Latin palette—though alas, it is now gone.

WINDOWS ON THE WORLD—the name tells the story of this crystal palace atop the World Trade Center, flooded with sunlight by day and up amongst the stars by night, where the tables are conceived like a series of amphitheaters and every seat shares in the breathtaking view of New York, 107 stories below.

CELLAR IN THE SKY—in a space without windows, light becomes
sculpture. It ripples, a moving thing, through walls of bottles, green,
amber, ruby, topaz jewels, glistening brilliantly.

And now, AURORA—Baum's own, very own realization of his dream,
named after the goddess of the dawn, which opened just this year and
has become an instant sensation.

Joe Baum describes light as his "trusty sidekick." "If I didn't know it
intuitively," he says, "then I stumbled on it, with the certainty of a barked
shin. Light literally *inspires* us. We draw in our breath. We gasp. Light
delights our minds and strengthens our will to do good, and to avoid evil."

I do not know whether people will avoid doing evil after they have
experienced the ambiance of Aurora; perhaps they will avoid doing it, at
least, while they are *there.* There is so much else to do of a happier sort,
and a suggestion of bubbles everywhere—floating across the ceiling in
pink and lavender, silver and rose—prompts a lightness of the heart. Look
closely and you find bubbles etched even in the crystal you hold in your
hand, and that prompts laughter.

Yellow-gold light dapples at midday through the latticed windows and
fills the room at night in a subtly changing borealis. The food is light,
elegant: a juxtaposition of brilliant innovation based on classic dishes and
simple grills. There is space, space to spare, a true indulgence in our times.
The realization: Baum himself, teamed with Milton Glaser, the renowned
graphics designer, and architect Philip George. For the exquisite food, the
bow goes to Gérard Pangaud, a young chef who brought two stars with
him from his native France.

Says Baum, of Aurora and all his work: "I am interested in a restaurant
that is enduringly built on the truth of the present, a restaurant that does
not lurch forward on unrelated novelties of the past, but rather is inspired
by honesty and built on the depth of experience."

"I lust after restaurants' drama, their ambiance, their professionalism—
and their glorious food," he says, describing his early recognition that a
really excellent restaurant not only endures, but prevails through fad after
fad. "It's the difference between liking what is new and loving what is
good," he believes. "A good restaurant takes a basic drive—the simple act
of eating—and transforms it into a civilized ritual involving hospitality and
imagination and satisfaction and graciousness and warmth."

Baum's ideal menu? "A loaf of bread, a jug of wine, and thou." "It's a
simple menu," he says, "but Omar Khayyam knew what he was doing. He
matched his menu to his requirements. And you don't always need
elaborate, complicated cuisine. As Jim Beard never tired of drumming into
me, 'taste is the greatest challenge of all. Taste is the only rule in this time
of freshness and freedom.' "

Many critics call Baum the greatest creator of restaurants in the 20th
century; certainly we feel his influence every time we walk into a
restaurant and are welcomed with warmth, space and style.

Baum's care shows in
every element of
Aurora's design, from
the entrance canopy
(remade again and again
until it had just the
right lightness and
color) to the warmly
welcoming interior with
its rosy baubles.

The Melting Pot

American Bistro has remade the menu and given us a lexicon of glorious alternatives. Why march through a meal in the old lockstep—appetizer, main course, dessert—when we can have our cake and eat it two, or even three times over?

American bistros set no pecking order for your dining. They will not force you to a table, unless you ask for one, and a comfortable perch always awaits you before the ample surface of the long, gleaming bar. There, with your companion, or a neighbor who, like you, enjoys the informality, you can create a menu of littlemeals and small snacks, and stay at the center of the swirling action.

Be audacious—and like the arrangement of this book, abandon the traditional formats. No one is saying you can't have a steamed vegetable plate, cholesterol-free, followed by a towering chocolate chip ice cream sundae with hot fudge sauce. Or, if you fancy, nibble at some deep-fried celery root or a slice of exquisitely striped pâté, or tuck into some cornmeal cakes

elevated to greatness with a dash of crème fraîche and a splash of caviar.

Why not make a meal from three appetizers and two desserts—or the reverse, with perhaps a salad to clear the palate? You can share every dish with your companions or even select from a special sampling menu. There is only one rule—that it is all right to eat when you feel like it.

Though there is still an important place for traditional dining patterns, today's relaxed, more impromptu lifestyles insist that they share the scene with a kind of eating based on movement, whimsy and uninhibited fun. Its origins, in fact, lie deep in the early years of this century, when most metropolitan bars offered the classic "free lunch"—gigantic, fragrant roasts from which slabs of beef and pork and lamb would be carved and slapped on chunks of rye bread, along with other tasty edibles, while the barmen pumped fountains of foaming beer into huge tankards. The patron was king—as long as he kept ordering an unending flow of the malty brew.

Bistros are at our end of that moving evolutionary line, and we are free citizens in these modern palaces. They may be a good bit grander, but they are still close enough to their forebears for us to be at liberty to select our fare in our own language, and to recognize with delight the features they have in common: abundance, energy and choice.

The power tea, with scones and tiny cakes, is "in" from Detroit to Dallas, where The Mansion on Turtle Creek (left) accompanies it with a little harp music. In New York the ethnic morsels being served at Orso's (above right) raise antipasto to a sublime level and Felipe Rojas-Lombardi (above left) offers such an array of tapas at The Ballroom that you could fancy yourself in Spain.

Moroccan Eggplant

Makes 8 tapas or appetizer servings
Preheat the oven to 500 degrees

4 long, plump eggplants,
   each weighing about 1¼ pounds
⅓–½ cup olive oil
3–4 bunches cilantro
   (about 6 ounces, to yield 3½ cups)
1 teaspoon finely chopped garlic
1 teaspoon finely chopped
   fresh ginger
1 teaspoon finely chopped
   and seeded fresh hot chili pepper
3–4 teaspoons lemon juice
1 teaspoon ground cumin
1–1¼ teaspoons coarse salt
Black pepper to taste
1 lemon, thinly sliced

Place a broiler pan in the middle of the oven.

Rinse and dry the eggplants, but do not trim them. Prick each in several places and rub lightly with olive oil. Bake them until they are tender, turning occasionally. (The timing can very considerably, from 15 to 35 minutes.) The skin will be blackened and slightly charred. Let the eggplants cool.

Rinse and dry the cilantro; trim the roots and some of the stems. Chop coarsely and measure 3½ cups. Combine 3 tablespoons of the oil in a blender or processor with the garlic, ginger and chili pepper and process until smooth. With the machine running, add 2 cups of the cilantro. Add a tablespoon of the lemon juice, the cumin, 1 teaspoon of the salt and 3 tablespoons of oil.

Add the remaining cilantro and process until the mixture is smooth. Taste and season, if needed, with salt, lemon juice and pepper. Add more olive oil, if necessary, to make a thick sauce which can be spooned in soft masses.

Peel the skin away from the eggplants gently, keeping them intact. Start at the stem and peel down. Without cutting through the stem, slice each into 4 or 5 thick, lengthwise slices. (They are too soft to make neat slices.) With a teaspoon and your fingers, gently scoop out as many seeds as possible. Fan out each eggplant and fit them together onto a serving platter.

Spoon the sauce decoratively between the slices and garnish with the lemon.

The Ballroom Tortilla Español

Makes 6–8 tapas or appetizer servings
4 lunch or light supper servings

4 large potatoes (about 1¾ pounds)
1 very large yellow onion
⅓ cup olive oil, preferably Spanish
⅓ cup vegetable oil
10 eggs
1–1¼ teaspoon salt
White pepper to taste

Tapas have long been a prized feature of Spanish cuisine and The Ballroom bar offers an almost overwhelming range of choices.

Peel the potatoes and the onion and cut them into fairly thin, even slices. Heat ¼ cup each of the olive and vegetable oils in a 12-inch non-stick skillet. Add the potatoes and onions; toss to separate the slices and coat them well with oil. Cook over moderate heat, stirring often, until the potatoes are tender but not browned, about 20 minutes.

Whisk the eggs, 1 teaspoon of salt and pepper to taste. Stirring constantly, add the hot potato and onion mixture. Let stand briefly and taste for salt and pepper. Wipe out the skillet, if needed.

Heat an additional 3 tablespoons of the combined oils in the skillet. Pour in the egg mixture and distribute evenly. Turn the heat to the lowest point, cover the pan and cook until the eggs are firm in the center, 15 to 20 minutes. (Some liquid will remain on the top.)

Invert the tortilla onto the skillet cover or a platter. Heat another tablespoon of oil in the skillet and slide in the tortilla, golden-brown side up. Cook for 4 to 5 minutes, until set underneath.

Let the tortilla stand 10 minutes, then slip it onto a serving dish and allow to cool to room temperature. Cut into wedges to serve.

Pulpo a la Gallega (Octopus in Paprika Sauce)

Makes 10 tapas or appetizer servings

6 quarts water
1 onion, peeled and quartered
6 bay leaves
12 cloves garlic, peeled
1-inch piece of fresh ginger,
   peeled and sliced
6 juniper berries
1 tablespoon coarse salt
3½ pounds fresh octopus,
   cleaned and separated
¼ cup olive oil, preferably Spanish
3 tablespoons flour
1 tablespoon Spanish paprika
½ teaspoon cayenne pepper

Combine the water, onion, 3 bay leaves, 4 garlic cloves, ginger, juniper berries and salt in a large pot; bring to a boil. Add the octopus, bring to a simmer and cook for about 1 hour, or until the octopus is very tender. Set it aside to cool briefly; reserve 2½ cups of the cooking liquid.

Run the octopus under warm water and rub off the dark layer of skin and some of the soft underlayer; leave the suction cups intact. Cut both pouch and tentacles into 1-inch pieces.

Heat the oil, remaining 3 bay leaves and 8 garlic cloves in a skillet over moderate heat. When the garlic is pale golden, remove the skillet from the heat and add the flour, paprika and cayenne, stirring with a whisk. Add the reserved cooking liquid. Bring to a boil, stirring. Lower the heat and simmer for 10 minutes, stirring often, until the sauce has thickened and no longer tastes floury. Remove the garlic; taste for salt and add the octopus. Stir to combine. Serve warm or at room temperature.

All three of these recipes are from Felipe Rojas-Lombardi, chef-owner of The Ballroom in New York City, the place where the current American craze for tapas first got started. Much of the credit for the popularity of these intensely flavored, hugely varied morsels is due to Felipe and his devoted staff, who make it a pleasure to drop into The Ballroom for a taste or two.

West Indian Potato-Shrimp Fritters with Salsa Cruda

Makes 18 bonbocca or fritters

Salsa Cruda:

1½ pounds ripe plum tomatoes, peeled, seeded and chopped
1 clove garlic, finely chopped
2 tablespoons finely chopped basil or cilantro, or both
Salt and pepper to taste
3–4 tablespoons flavorful olive oil

Fritters:

2 baking potatoes (about 1¼ pounds), peeled and quartered
8 tablespoons butter
¾ cup finely chopped onion
1 pound shrimp, peeled and deveined
1 cup grated mild white cheddar cheese
1 egg yolk
2 tablespoons finely chopped cilantro
2 tablespoons finely chopped parsley
1 teaspoon salt
½ teaspoon pepper
½ cup flour
2 eggs, beaten
2½ cups soft, fresh breadcrumbs
Vegetable oil for deep-frying

Prepare the salsa: Combine the tomatoes, garlic, basil and/or cilantro, and salt and pepper to taste. Stir in the olive oil. Cover and set aside until serving time.

Boil the potatoes until tender. Melt half the butter in a skillet and stir in the onions. Cook over low heat, stirring occasionally, until translucent, about 10 minutes. Add the shrimp and toss until almost but not completely pink. Transfer to the bowl of a food processor.

Drain the potatoes thoroughly. Mash them in a bowl with a fork or a potato masher. Add the remaining butter to the potatoes and mash well. Mash in the cheese, egg yolk, cilantro, parsley, salt and pepper.

Pulse the food processor a few times to chop the shrimp and onion into small pieces. Add to the mashed potatoes and mix thoroughly. Cover and chill for at least an hour.

Scoop up a scant ¼ cup of the chilled mixture, form it into a neat cake about 1 inch thick and set on a baking sheet covered with wax paper. Form about 18 cakes. Coat each one lightly with flour, then dip into the beaten eggs. Cover each completely with the soft crumbs and replace on the wax paper. When all the cakes have been coated, refrigerate them at least 30 minutes.

Heat vegetable oil to 375 degrees in a deep-fat fryer or an electric skillet. Fry 2 or 3 fritters at a time until deeply golden, about 2 to 2½ minutes. Drain on paper towels. Serve hot, with a few spoonfuls of the salsa alongside.

Yvonne Bell, Lola's co-owner and guiding light, presides at a bar laden with her restaurant's specialties— tempting "bonbocca," West Indian/Caribbean for "good mouthful." And indeed they are.

Eggplant and Prosciutto "Sandwiches"

Makes 16 bonbocca or "sandwiches"

2 eggplants, each about
   8 inches long and weighing
   about 1 pound
2 teaspoons coarse salt
¼ pound thinly sliced prosciutto
½ pound mozzarella cheese
16 large fresh sage leaves
Vegetable oil for frying
1 cup flour
4 eggs, beaten
1¼ cups yellow cornmeal

Cut off the top and base of each eggplant and slice into rounds ⅛ to ¼ inch thick. There should be about 32 even, good-sized slices. Layer the slices in a large bowl, sprinkling them evenly with the salt. Place a dish or plate on the eggplant and top with a weight of 2 to 3 pounds. Let stand an hour or so. Rinse very quickly, then press as much liquid as possible from the slices. Put them between sheets of paper towel and press again to dry.

Place half the eggplant on a working surface. Put a prosciutto slice, folded or cut to fit, on each eggplant round. Cut the cheese into as many slices as needed and place one on each piece of ham. Top with the sage, then another eggplant slice. Press down to flatten each sandwich.

Heat oil to a depth of ½ inch in a 12-inch skillet. Dredge each sandwich in flour, coat thoroughly with egg, then roll in the cornmeal to cover completely.

Fry about 5 at a time over moderate heat. Turn the sandwiches over when golden, about 2 minutes. Fry until light brown. Drain on paper towels and serve hot.

Two recipes from Lola, a friendly peach-colored restaurant in New York's Chelsea district. The golden-brown, crisp fritters are plump and attractive, with their bright, sharp garnish. The thin coating, broken with a fork, reveals a creamy, puffy puree studded with shrimp and herbs. The meltingly tender "sandwiches" can be prepared ahead without their coating, refrigerated, then dipped and fried at the very last minute.

29

Red Pepper and Eggplant Terrine

Serves 8
Preheat the oven to 350 degrees

2 medium eggplants (about 2 pounds total)
Salt
8 medium-size red bell peppers
½ cup extra-virgin olive oil

Peel the eggplants and cut them across into ⅛-inch-thick slices. Lightly salt the slices and let them drain in a colander for 30 minutes.

Pat the eggplant dry, then layer the slices between paper towels. Cover them with a cookie sheet and weight with a heavy pot for 1 hour.

Halve, core and seed the peppers and place them in a roasting pan in a single layer, cut side down. Drizzle with ⅓ cup of the olive oil. Roast the peppers until the skins are wrinkled and loose, 30 to 40 minutes. Remove them from the oven and let stand until they are cool enough to handle. Peel away the skins and discard them. Tip the roasting pan and pour the oil and juices into a bowl and reserve.

Place a large skillet over moderately high heat. Dip a paper towel into the remaining oil and very lightly grease the skillet. When the skillet is hot, add a single layer of eggplant slices and cook 2 to 3 minutes on each side, until they are tender and lightly browned. Drain on paper towels. Oil the skillet very lightly between batches, if needed; take care not to let the eggplant absorb too much oil.

Use the reserved oil and pepper juices to coat a stainless steel or glass loaf pan, 6 by 3 by 2 inches. Line the bottom and sides with slightly overlapping eggplant slices, pressing them into the corners to form a rectangular shape. Cover with an even layer of red peppers, pressing them into corners and cutting pieces to fit as needed. Continue layering eggplant and peppers until the pan is filled, ending with a layer of eggplant.

Bake the terrine for 30 minutes. Use paper towels to blot any liquid that has accumulated on top of the terrine during baking. Cover the terrine with plastic wrap and weight it with a loaf pan of the same size filled with rice or beans. Let it cool to room temperature. Blot any oil that rises to the surface. Refrigerate the weighted terrine overnight or for as long as 3 days.

Unmold the terrine and cut into 8 equal slices with a sharp, thin knife.

This is the food of our times—strikingly beautiful, and tasty, too. Chefs today are not only skilled cooks but artists—even though, moments later, their creation is only an aroma hovering in the air. Yet we remember it, and want it again, and again.

Herbed Chicken Pâté with Mustard Crème Fraîche

Serves 8 as an appetizer
Preheat the oven to 350 degrees

1 pound boned, skinned chicken breasts
1 egg
2 tablespoons chopped fresh dill
1½ tablespoons chopped chives
1½ tablespoons finely chopped fresh tarragon
1¼ teaspoons salt
¼ teaspoon nutmeg
⅛ teaspoon cayenne pepper
1½ cups heavy cream
2 tablespoons Dijon mustard
¾ cup crème fraîche

Remove any membrane, tendons, or pieces of fat from the chicken; cut the meat into 1-inch pieces. Place in the bowl of a food processor with the egg, dill, chives, tarragon, salt, nutmeg and cayenne. Process the mixture to a fine consistency.

With the motor running, add the cream in a slow, steady stream. As soon as it is incorporated, transfer the mixture to an oiled 9-by-5-by-3-inch loaf pan; it will be about half filled. Smooth the top of the mixture, then cover it with a piece of oiled foil. Set the loaf in a larger pan and pour enough boiling water in to come about halfway up the sides of the loaf pan.

Place the pâté in the preheated oven and bake until it reaches a temperature of 150 degrees in the center, about 45 to 50 minutes. Remove the pan from the water bath and uncover. Let the pâté cool to lukewarm. Run a knife around the edges. Invert onto a plate and refrigerate. The pâté can be prepared a day ahead.

Combine the mustard and the crème fraîche and chill until serving time. Cut the pâté into ¼-inch slices about an hour before serving and let stand at room temperature. Serve with a generous dollop of sauce.

A recipe from Laura Thorne, chef at The Coast Grill, a favored spot in the Hamptons, summer haven for New Yorkers. Serve it on brightly colored plates or a bed of dark greens.

A Cheesecake Made with Smoked Salmon, Leeks and Wild Mushrooms

Serves 12
Preheat the oven to 300 degrees

7 tablespoons butter
1 cup chopped leeks
¼ cup sliced shiitake mushroom caps
1½ pounds cream cheese
3 egg yolks
1 tablespoon cornstarch
⅓ cup heavy cream
⅔ pound smoked salmon
½ cup grated Gruyère cheese
1 teaspoon salt
½ teaspoon freshly ground black pepper
½ cup breadcrumbs
½ cup grated Parmesan cheese

Heat 3 tablespoons of the butter in a skillet and cook the leeks over moderate heat for about 3 minutes; raise the heat, add the mushrooms and cook, stirring constantly, for about 4 minutes. Transfer the mixture to a plate and let it cool slightly.

Combine the cream cheese, egg yolks, cornstarch and cream in a mixer and beat until smooth.

Remove any tiny bones from the salmon, then cut it into small pieces. Combine it with the leeks and mushrooms, the Gruyere and the cream cheese mixture. Add the salt and pepper and mix very well.

Mix the breadcrumbs and Parmesan and set aside 3 tablespoons of the mixture.

Generously butter a 9-inch terrine or loaf pan with the remaining 4 tablespoons of butter. Line the terrine with the crumb mixture, patting it into place to make it adhere to the sides.

Fill the terrine with the cheesecake mixture and sprinkle the top with the reserved crumbs. Place it in a roasting pan and pour 2 inches of boiling water into the pan. Bake in the preheated oven for 1½ hours. Turn off the heat and let the cake sit in the oven, with the door ajar, for 1 hour. Remove the cake and let cool to room temperature, then refrigerate it for 12 hours or longer.

To unmold, surround the pan with a hot moist towel and invert.

The cake must be very cold to slice well, but tastes best at cool room temperature. Therefore, slice it and arrange on serving plates an hour or so before serving.

Two very rich and subtle recipes: a smoked salmon cheesecake from Richard Perry's Restaurant in St. Louis and a scallop mousse from Quatorze, a bistro in the heart of New York's meat district.

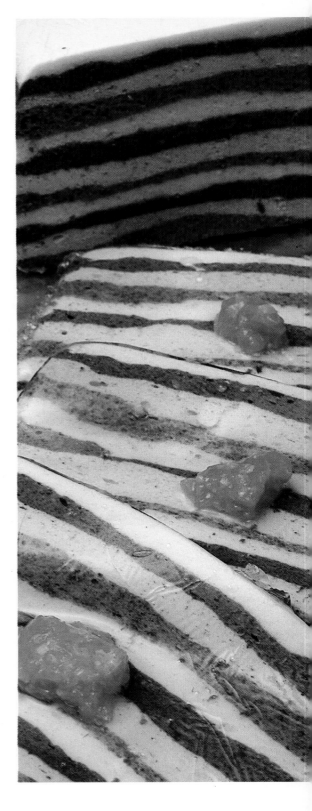

Urban time out: today's paper, a glass of wine and a slice of exquisite pate.

Scallop Mousse

Serves 6 as an appetizer
Preheat the oven to 350 degrees

9 ounces bay scallops
½ teaspoon salt
⅛ teaspoon white pepper
¼ teaspoon grated lemon rind
1 egg white
1 cup heavy cream
1 tablespoon butter
1 cup Beurre Blanc, page 168
¼ teaspoon saffron threads

Rinse, dry and trim the scallops, removing any hard pieces of connective tissue. Place them in the container of a food processor, along with the salt, pepper and lemon rind. Process until the scallops are smooth, scraping down the sides as needed. Add the egg white and blend for 30 seconds.

With the machine running, pour in the cream in a steady stream, stopping once to scrape down the sides. Process just long enough to incorporate the cream; do not warm up the mixture by over-processing.

Butter 6 ½-cup molds or custard cups and divide the mixture among them. Tap down the mousse and smooth the tops. Set the molds in a pan, cover with plastic, and chill for an hour or longer.

Uncover the pan and pour in boiling water to come halfway up the sides of the molds. Bake in the center of the oven for about 20 to 25 minutes, or until the mousse is slightly puffed and firm in the center.

While the mousse bakes, prepare the Beurre Blanc. As you stir in the final half of the butter, add the saffron, reserving a few strands for garnish.

Remove the mousse from the water bath and let it stand about 10 minutes before serving. Run a knife around the edge, pour off any accumulated liquid, then invert each onto a small warm serving plate. Cover with a few spoonfuls of Beurre Blanc and sprinkle sparingly with the reserved saffron.

Smoked Swordfish

Brine:

4 quarts water
1 box table salt (1 pound, 4 ounces)
½ cup light brown sugar
6 small dried chili peppers,
 crumbled
20 black peppercorns, bruised
3–4 bay leaves

7–8 pounds swordfish, cut into
 1-inch-thick slices

Porgies grilled over mesquite are finished with bright zigzags of red pepper puree, a signature of the new American cooking, and presented on glistening stones, which may be a flight of nouvelle photographic fancy.

When you are going to the trouble of using a smoker, it is worthwhile to brine and smoke fish in large quantities.

Combine the ingredients for the brine in a large pot and bring to a boil. Boil for 15 minutes. Strain the brine and let cool.

Soak the swordfish in the brine for 1 hour, then rinse and dry it. Remove the rack from the smoker and arrange the fish on it. Place an electric fan 2 feet from the fish and blow the air onto it for about 15 minutes on one side; then reverse the rack and continue for another 15 minutes. This drying will seal the surface of the fish and give it a glossy finish, called the pellicle.

While the fish is drying, start the smoker, using alder chips with one big chunk of mesquite to keep the fire going.

Cover the smoker box and, in about 30 minutes, when it is warm and full of smoke, put in the rack with the pellicled fish.

Replenish the fuel pan as the woods burn; 3 refills is the average.

The time needed will vary with the weather and with how well protected the smoker is. In mild weather, the fish will be smoked in 4 to 5 hours, but on cold days it will take about 18 hours.

The Indians of the Pacific Northwest liked to use alder chips to smoke the salmon that were so plentiful in their rivers, thereby preserving them tastily for later use. Alder and similar hardwood chips also make a good smoke for swordfish, as this recipe proves.

Smoked Swordfish Salad

Serves 2–4

½ cup mayonnaise
2 teaspoons fresh lemon juice
Freshly ground pepper
1½ teaspoons chopped fresh rosemary
1 small carrot, grated
¼ cup finely chopped celery
¼ cup finely chopped onion
2 hard-cooked eggs, chopped
2 cups cubed smoked swordfish
Red lettuce, for garnish

Combine all of the ingredients and serve on red lettuce.

At Under the Blue Moon in Philadelphia, the owners, Phyllis and Eugene Gosfield, provide a variety of on-the-premises smoked meats and fish. The end product of this treatment is so good that it requires little else in the way of effort. This salad is a good example.

Cured Salmon

Serves 10–12

Salmon:

½ cup clear or sea rock salt
1 cup sugar
2 tablespoons cracked white pepper
1 cup chopped fresh dill
2 1-inch-thick salmon fillets (about 2 pounds)
3 tablespoons aquavit

Sauce:

¼ cup Dijon mustard
1 tablespoon white wine vinegar
1½ teaspoons sugar
½ cup peanut oil
1 tablespoon chopped fresh dill
Salt and freshly ground pepper

Butter lettuce leaves
Lemon wedges

Combine the salt, sugar and pepper in a bowl, tossing to blend. Spread a quarter of the salt mixture in the bottom of a deep dish and sprinkle with one-third of the dill. Place a piece of salmon, skin side down, on the dill. Rub the flesh side with 1 tablespoon of aquavit. Sprinkle with a quarter of the salt mixture and half the remaining dill, then sprinkle half the remaining salt mixture over the dill. Rub the flesh side of the second salmon fillet with 1 tablespoon of aquavit. Place the salmon on top of the first piece of fish, skin side up. Rub it with the last of the aquavit and sprinkle with what is left of the salt and dill.

Cover the salmon with a sheet of kitchen parchment or wax paper and a plate, to hold it in place without weighting the salmon too heavily. Let the dish rest at room temperature for 2 hours. Refrigerate, with the plate in place, for 48 hours. Turn the entire "sandwich" of salmon, cover it again with the parchment and plate, and refrigerate for 24 hours more.

Remove the salmon fillets and scrape off the salt and dill. Discard the curing marinade. The salmon is now ready to serve, but it can be wrapped in plastic and refrigerated for up to a week.

To make the sauce, combine the mustard, vinegar and sugar in a small bowl. Beat in the oil, a little at a time, stirring constantly with a whisk. Stir in the dill, and salt and pepper to taste. There will be about ¾ cup.

Cut the salmon on the bias into paper-thin slices. Serve on lettuce leaves with a tablespoon of sauce and a wedge of lemon.

A sublime version of gravlax with a wonderfully creamy sauce from Uffe Gustafsson, chef at Bentley's oyster bar in San Francisco.

Smoked Goose Breast with Cranberry Walnut Mayonnaise

Serves 4

Sauce:

1 tablespoon finely chopped fresh cranberries
1 tablespoon finely chopped walnuts
2 teaspoons Dijon mustard
1 teaspoon grated horseradish
1 drop Worcestershire sauce
1 drop hot pepper sauce
Salt and freshly ground white pepper
⅔ cup freshly made mayonnaise

4 grape leaves
½ pound thinly sliced smoked goose breast
   or smoked turkey breast
12 red apple slices
12 green apple slices

Mix all the ingredients for the sauce and refrigerate for 2 hours or longer, to let the flavors develop.

   Just before serving, place a grape leaf on a medium-sized plate and fan out one-fourth of the goose slices near the top of the leaf. Fan 6 apple slices at the stem end of the leaf, alternating the colors. Set a heaping spoonful of the mayonnaise between the apples and goose, in the center of the leaf. Repeat 3 times and serve immediately.

A colorful conceit served at the American Restaurant in Kansas City.

The mesquite most of us know only in the form of aromatic wood chips spreads leafy green boughs in the arid lands of the Sonoran desert. In San Francisco's Café Americain, below, purity of the food on the plate is considered as carefully as the height of the benches— everything is to scale.

Along with the special of the day, we now must choose the wood of the day. Shall our fare be grilled over mesquite, oak or grape twigs?

Skirt Steak with Soy and Ginger Marinade

Serves 6
Prepare a fire for grilling

6 cloves garlic, coarsely chopped
3 ounces fresh ginger, peeled and
  coarsely chopped (about ⅔ cup)
¼ cup dark soy sauce
¼ cup dry sherry
¼ cup rice wine vinegar
¼ cup olive oil
2 tablespoons Oriental sesame oil
6 skirt steaks, about 8 ounces
  each, trimmed of fat

Combine the garlic, ginger, soy, sherry, vinegar and oils in a large, ceramic or enamel bowl. Add the steaks and turn to coat them with the marinade. Cover and marinate for 1 hour at room temperature or up to 8 hours in the refrigerator. If they are refrigerated, return them to room temperature before cooking.

Scrape the garlic and ginger from the meat and pat it dry with paper towels. Grill the steaks about 4 inches from the heat, turning once, for about 3 minutes on each side for rare or 4 minutes per side for medium-rare.

Transfer from the grill to a carving board and let rest, loosely covered, for 10 minutes before carving. Cut on the diagonal into thin slices.

A fine use (pictured below) of an underappreciated cut of beef by Chef Cindy Pawlcyn of Mustards Grill in the Napa Valley.

Marinated Baby Chicken with Fresh Garden Relish

Serves 4

4 poussins or Cornish hens,
  each 1¼ pounds
3–4 teaspoons fresh rosemary leaves
2 garlic cloves, sliced
½ cup fresh lemon juice
1 cup light vegetable oil
3 medium-size tomatoes (1 pound)
1 medium-size cucumber
½ medium-size red onion
2 jalapeño peppers, finely chopped
2 tablespoons finely chopped cilantro
2–3 tablespoons balsamic vinegar
2–3 tablespoons olive oil
Salt and freshly ground pepper to taste

Cut out the backbone of each bird. Flatten them and place in a non-corrodible dish.

Bruise the rosemary gently with a knife to release the oils. Combine it with the garlic, lemon juice and vegetable oil and pour over the birds. Cover the dish and refrigerate for 12 to 24 hours, turning occasionally.

Quarter the tomatoes and remove the stems, cores and seeds. Cut the shells into ¼-inch dice. Peel the cucumber if it is waxed. Seed and dice it and combine with the tomatoes in a bowl. Add the onion, jalapeños, cilantro, 2 tablespoons each of the vinegar and olive oil, and salt and pepper to taste. Cover and let the relish stand several hours. Taste and adjust the seasonings. The relish can be prepared ahead and refrigerated; let it come to room temperature before serving.

Prepare a fire made from an equal quantity of charcoal briquettes and mesquite, or preheat the oven to 425 degrees.

Let the birds come to room temperature and remove them from the marinade. Pat them dry and sprinkle with salt and pepper.

Grill until golden over a fairly low fire, or roast in the oven for about 25 minutes.

Serve the birds hot or at room temperature, with the relish.

In Lavin's Restaurant, New York, these quantities serve four; they will also feed eight svelte friends beautifully.

Grilled Shrimp with Tomato-Dill Butter

Serves 4 as an appetizer
Prepare a charcoal fire or preheat the broiler

1 cup fresh tomato puree
   or ½ cup, canned
¾ cup dry vermouth or
   very dry white wine
2 teaspoons finely chopped shallots
9 tablespoons butter
2½ tablespoons chopped fresh dill
Salt and freshly ground pepper
12 jumbo shrimp
Autumn Salad, page 134

Combine the tomato puree, vermouth and shallots in a non-corrodible saucepan. Cook over moderate heat until the liquid is reduced to ¾ cup, if you are using fresh puree, or to about ½ cup, if you are using the canned. Remove the pan from the heat and beat in the butter, a little at a time, adding new butter as the old is incorporated. Stir in the dill and season with salt and pepper to taste.

Shell and devein the shrimp. Season with salt and pepper and grill for 2 minutes on each side, for a total of about 4 minutes. Let them rest for a minute and then split each in half, lengthwise.

Pour 3 tablespoons of the Tomato-Dill Butter onto each of 4 warm plates and spread the sauce so that the entire center of the plate is covered. Place a serving of Autumn Salad in the center and arrange 6 shrimp halves around the salad.

The Fifth Avenue Grill makes California-style cuisine in the heart of New York City, and this recipe from Chef John Schenk has all the virtues we attribute to the West Coast.

Grilled Squab Marinated in Berry Puree

Serves 4
Prepare a charcoal fire

4 squab
2½ cups fresh raspberries
¼ pound butter
Salt and freshly ground pepper
4 tablespoons olive oil
½ pound salt pork, cut into 1-inch-by-¼-inch pieces
1 tablespoon chopped fresh thyme
16 mushrooms
2 tablespoons freshly squeezed lemon juice
½ cup walnut oil
3 bunches watercress, trimmed, washed and dried

Remove the livers and hearts from the squab and reserve. Slit the birds down the back, cut out the backbone, flatten them and fold the wings under.

Select 24 raspberries for decoration and puree the rest by hand, rubbing them through a sieve. Divide the puree in half, mixing one-half into the butter, with salt and pepper, in a food processor. Add 2 tablespoons of the olive oil to the remaining raspberry puree. Season the birds with salt and pepper and cover with the oil-puree marinade. Let marinate for 1 hour.

Blanch the salt pork and rinse and drain it. Trim the squab livers. Mix the remaining 2 tablespoons of olive oil with the chopped thyme and rub into the salt pork, livers, hearts and mushrooms and let marinate for 45 minutes. Divide these ingredients evenly among 4 skewers.

Grill the squab, breast side down, for 8 minutes. Move them occasionally to ensure even cooking. Turn them to the other side and grill for about 10 minutes. Remove from the grill and let them rest for 5 minutes before serving. While the squab are resting, grill the filled skewers for 5 minutes, turning them frequently.

Mix the lemon juice and walnut oil in a bowl and season with salt and pepper. Toss with the watercress and divide it among hot plates. Put the squab in the center of each plate and encircle with the salt pork, livers, hearts and mushrooms. Turn the reserved raspberries in any vinaigrette still coating the bowl and scatter them around each plate. Put some of the raspberry butter on top of each bird and serve.

Trained as an architect, Jeremiah Tower found his vocation as a chef, and his influence is far-reaching. He attributes the inspiration for this recipe to a 17th-century cookbook, but his treatment is totally contemporary—and marvelous.

Chardonnay prunings in hand, Jeremiah Tower, the star of California cooking, stops on his way to the grill at Stars, San Francisco.

Diners at Atwater's in Portland, Oregon, are welcomed by two splendid Chinese lions to the peach-colored comfort beyond.

Goat cheese has become one of the hallmarks of the new American cooking. Equally welcome hot or cold, it turns up in an incredible variety of roles. At left is a classic favorite, slices of creamy cheese sprinkled with fresh herbs and drizzled with fruity extra-virgin olive oil. Below are those who make it all happen.

Whole Roasted Peppers with Ricotta and Goat Cheese

Serves 6–8
Preheat the broiler

¾ cup small curd cottage cheese
4 small bell peppers
   (preferably assorted colors)
½ cup ricotta cheese
¼ cup goat cheese
½ cup freshly grated Parmesan cheese
1 teaspoon fresh thyme leaves
1 tablespoon finely chopped parsley
1 tablespoon finely chopped red onion
Salt and freshly ground pepper
Watercress for garnish

Put the cottage cheese in a sieve and let it drain in the refrigerator for about 2 hours.

Roast the whole peppers under the broiler or over a gas flame, turning them frequently, until they are blackened on all sides. Blacken them as quickly as possible so as not to overcook and soften them. Rinse the peppers under gently running cold water to remove the charred skin; core and seed them and pat dry with paper towels.

Rub the drained cottage cheese through the sieve and into a bowl. Add the remaining cheeses, herbs, onion and salt and pepper to taste, and mix well.

Fill each pepper in turn with the cheese mixture and set it in a coffee cup to hold it upright. Refrigerate for at least 4 hours, until the filling is firm.

To serve, cut the peppers across into fairly thin slices and serve 3 or 4 to each person. For best results, dip the knife blade in hot water before cutting each slice. Garnish each plate with a sprig of watercress.

At The Trellis in Williamsburg, Virginia, Chef Marcel Desaulniers often serves these with toasted hazelnut bread.

California Pizzelle

Serves 4–8
Preheat the oven to 500 degrees

½ pound small shiitake mushrooms
2 tablespoons olive oil, preferably
   from California
1 clove garlic, finely chopped
½–⅔ cup very soft, fresh goat cheese,
   such as Laura Chenel's California
   Chèvre Fromage Blanc
4 flour (not corn) tortillas,
   about 8 inches in diameter
¼ cup chopped sun-dried tomatoes,
   drained of their oil
½ cup grated Monterey Jack cheese,
   lightly packed (about 2 ounces)

Set 2 old baking sheets (not good ones, which may warp) on the oven floor, or use foil pans.

Remove and reserve the shiitake stems for another use. Cut the caps into thin slices. Heat the olive oil in a skillet and sauté the mushrooms over moderate heat until they are lightly cooked, about 2 minutes. Add the garlic and toss for a minute over low heat. Set the pan aside.

Spread one-fourth of the goat cheese in a thin, even layer on a tortilla, leaving a 1-inch margin. Distribute the shiitake and tomatoes over this, then top with the jack cheese. Repeat 3 times.

Place the tortillas on the heated baking sheets and replace them in the oven. Bake the tortillas for 1½ to 2 minutes, until the rims turn very light golden and the cheese begins to melt. Cut each little pizza in 6 wedges, using a pastry wheel. Serve immediately.

Flavorful, easy and surprisingly neat finger food from Chef John Pawula of Stephanie's Restaurant in Peoria, Illinois.

Avocado Blini

Makes 12–18 blini

2 eggs, lightly beaten
⅔ cup flour
½ teaspoon salt
3–4 tablespoons milk
Pulp of 1 ripe avocado (about 5 ounces), pureed
2–4 tablespoons butter, melted

Combine the eggs, flour, salt, milk and avocado. Stir until they are well blended. The mixture will be fairly thick, like cornbread batter.

Lightly butter and then heat a griddle or skillet. For each blini, use ¼ cup of batter and spread it out on the griddle into a circle about 3 inches in diameter. Cook over medium-low heat for about 1 minute on each side, until golden brown. The blini will still be moist within, rather like guacamole with a crust. Repeat until you have cooked all the batter.

At the Pawleys Island Inn in Pawleys Island, South Carolina, chef-owner Louis Osteen serves these guacamole-in-a-crust cakes as an appetizer, accompanied by warmed fresh crab or lobster meat. The blini have melted butter poured onto them, then the seafood is placed on top and sprinkled with fresh chives or chervil. Mmmm . . . .

Corn Pancakes from Charley's 517

Makes about 8 4-inch pancakes

½ cup milk
½ teaspoon dry yeast
¾ teaspoon sugar
1 egg, beaten
2 tablespoons butter, melted
⅛ teaspoon salt
2 tablespoons flour
½ cup yellow cornmeal,
  preferably stone-ground
Clarified butter or corn oil

Heat the milk until it is slightly hotter than lukewarm. Put the yeast and sugar into a bowl and add the warm milk.

Place the remaining ingredients in the container of a food processor. Add the milk mixture and process until smooth. Put the batter into a bowl and cover with plastic wrap. Let it rest for about an hour in a warm spot.

Lightly butter or oil a griddle, or use a non-stick skillet. Heat the pan and when it is hot, pour in sufficient batter to make a pancake about 4 inches in diameter. Cook the pancake, turning once, until golden on both sides. Repeat until you have used the batter.

These are the light, fluffy Corn Pancakes called for in—but by no means confined to—Chicken with Ancho Chili Sauce, page 58, the inspiration of Chef Bruce Auden at Charley's 517 in Houston, and another splendid example of the current passion for tiny cakes.

Cornmeal Pancakes from An American Place

Makes about 24 9-inch pancakes

1 cup flour
1 cup stone-ground cornmeal
¼ teaspoon salt
Freshly ground pepper
2 eggs
2 egg yolks
2 cups milk
4 tablespoons salted butter, melted
2 tablespoons finely chopped parsley
Clarified butter or corn oil

Mix the flour, cornmeal, salt, pepper, eggs and egg yolks. Gradually whisk in the milk and continue stirring until the batter is smooth.

Heat the butter in a saucepan until it foams and turns a light nutty brown; do not let it burn. Pour it into the batter and mix well. Stir in the parsley.

Let the batter rest for at least 30 minutes, or preferably, overnight.

Lightly brush a 9-inch crêpe pan with the clarified butter or oil. Heat the pan and pour in about 2 tablespoons of batter to coat the bottom. If the batter does not easily cover the bottom of the pan, thin it with a little milk. Cook the crêpe over medium heat for about 1 minute, or until lightly browned. Flip the pancake and cook the other side, for just a few seconds. Repeat until you have used the batter.

You will need a half-cup of the pancake batter and four of the finished cakes when you make these Cornmeal Pancakes as part of Larry Forgione's recipe for Barbecued Duck with Tomato-Chili Salsa, page 54; but I would recommend making them all up—just in case. I also prophesy that when you have made them once, you will find yourself wanting to make them and eat them out of hand.

Deep-Dish Spinach Pizza

Makes a 9-inch deep-dish pizza

Whole Wheat Pizza Dough:

1 package dry yeast
1 cup warm water
2 tablespoons olive oil
3 cups flour
1 cup whole wheat flour
2 teaspoons coarse salt

Pizza filling:

1 tablespoon olive oil
1 clove garlic, finely chopped
1 pound fresh spinach, cooked,
  squeezed dry and chopped
½ recipe Whole Wheat Pizza Dough
1½ cups shredded mozzarella cheese
¾ cup freshly grated Swiss cheese
⅓ cup freshly grated Parmesan cheese
1¼ cups thick tomato sauce
2 ripe plum tomatoes,
  cut into thin lengthwise slices
16 fresh basil leaves
1 small green pepper, cored,
  seeded and sliced into thin strips
1 small red pepper, cored,
  seeded and sliced into thin strips

Dissolve the yeast in warm water; stir in the olive oil and set it aside.

Combine the flours and salt in a food processor and process briefly. With the machine running, slowly pour in the yeast mixture through the feed tube and process until a firm, smooth and elastic ball of dough forms. If the dough is too dry, add another tablespoon or so of warm water; if it is too soft, add a little more flour.

Wrap the dough in plastic and refrigerate for at least 20 minutes, or up to one day.

Preheat the oven to 475 degrees.

Heat the 1 tablespoon of olive oil in a skillet. Add the garlic and sauté for 30 seconds. Add the spinach and stir to coat with the oil and garlic. Remove the skillet from the heat.

Lightly oil a 9-inch round baking pan which is 1½ inches deep. Roll the dough into a 12-inch circle and fit it into the pan. The dough should just cover the bottom and sides of the pan, with no overhang.

Mix the 3 cheeses together and spread 1½ cups of the mixture in the bottom of the pan. Spread the tomato sauce over the cheese, covering it completely. Spread the spinach over the tomato sauce, breaking up any clumps with a fork.

Arrange alternating slices of tomatoes and basil leaves around the edge of the pan, over the spinach. Fill the center with tomato slices, then arrange alternating strips of green and red pepper in a spoke fashion on the tomatoes. Sprinkle with the remaining cheeses.

Bake in the preheated oven for 25 minutes, until the cheese and crust are golden and the filling is bubbly. Remove from the oven and allow to sit for 5 minutes before cutting.

Prosciutto Pizza

Makes 4 8-inch pizzas

Pizza dough:

3 cups flour
1 package dry yeast
1 teaspoon salt
1 tablespoon clover honey
2 tablespoons olive oil
¾–1 cup water

Pizza topping:

5 tablespoons extra-virgin olive oil
1 teaspoon crushed red pepper flakes
½ pound fresh mozzarella cheese,
   preferably buffalo milk
½ pound Italian fontina cheese
2 small red peppers, cored, seeded
   and cut into thin strips
4 cloves garlic, unpeeled
¼ cup chopped fresh basil
   or 2 teaspoons dried
6 ounces thinly sliced prosciutto,
   julienned
1 red onion, thinly sliced
6 plum tomatoes, thinly sliced
6 ounces mild goat cheese such as
   Montrachet or Bûcheron, crumbled

Combine the flour and yeast in a food processor and process briefly.

Combine the salt, honey, olive oil and ¾ cup of water in a small bowl and mix well.

With the motor running, slowly pour the liquid through the feed tube and process until the dough forms a ball on the blade. Use more water if needed. Transfer the dough to a lightly floured surface and knead until it is smooth. Place it in an oiled bowl and allow to rest, covered, for 30 minutes.

Divide the dough into 4 equal parts and roll each piece into a smooth, tight ball. Place the dough on a baking sheet, cover with a damp towel and refrigerate up to 6 hours.

One hour before baking, remove the dough from the refrigerator and let it come to room temperature.

Lightly flour a work surface. Using the fleshy part of your fingertips, flatten each ball of dough into a circle approximately 6 inches in diameter, leaving the outer edge thicker than the center. Lift the dough from the work surface and gently stretch the edges, working clockwise, to form an 8-inch circle. Place each circle on a pizza paddle or baking sheet.

Preheat the oven to 500 degrees.

Combine 4 tablespoons of the extra-virgin olive oil and the crushed red pepper and let stand.

Grate the fontina and mozzarella cheeses into a bowl and mix thoroughly.

Heat the remaining oil in a heavy skillet and cook the red peppers until they soften, about 3 minutes.

Blanch the garlic in a pan of boiling water for 4 minutes; drain and peel it, then cut into paper-thin slices.

Brush the dough circles with the red pepper oil and sprinkle them with the basil. Spread an even layer of the cheeses on the basil and layer the peppers, garlic, prosciutto and onion on top. Finish with the tomato slices and then the crumbled goat cheese.

Bake the pizzas in the preheated oven until the crusts are golden brown and the tops are bubbly, about 20 minutes.

Wolfgang Puck (left) has befriended us all by bringing "designer pizza," just about single-handedly, into the purlieus of haute cuisine, and his restaurant, Spago's, in Los Angeles has become renowned as the showcase for his zestful, trend-setting approach to the new American cooking. The pizza above is already a classic. Opposite: a variation on the Chicago deep-dish pizza from Pizzapiazza, on lower Broadway in New York City, a haunt of students and sophisticates appealed to by its fine wine list and good food at fair prices.

Forest Fettuccine with Morels and Breast of Pheasant

Serves 4

Fettuccine:

½ ounce dried morels or 2
    tablespoons morel powder
¾ cup semolina flour
¾ cup all-purpose flour
2 extra-large eggs
2 extra-large egg yolks
1 tablespoon olive oil

Morel cream sauce:

18 dried morels (or fresh if in season)
1 tablespoon butter
2 tablespoons chopped shallots
1¾ cups heavy cream
Salt, white pepper and nutmeg to taste

Garnish:

24 fiddlehead ferns or asparagus tips
2 tablespoons butter

Breasts of two 3-pound pheasants,
    boned, skinned and halved
Salt and white pepper
2 tablespoons butter

Prepare the fettuccine. Clean any soil clinging to the morel stems. Place the mushrooms in a spice mill and grind to a fine powder. Combine the powder with the semolina and all-purpose flours in a food processor and process briefly to blend. Beat the eggs, egg yolks and oil together and, with the motor running, add the mixture to the flours. Process until a neat ball forms on top of the blade, about 45 to 60 seconds. Remove the dough from the machine and knead for a minute on a very lightly floured surface. Pat into a thick cylinder and wrap it in plastic. Refrigerate for at least 1 hour.

About 1 hour before serving time, cut the dough across into 6 pieces. Knead, stretch, and cut each piece in a pasta machine or by hand. Spread the fettuccine on a tray dusted with semolina. Cover with a towel until cooking time.

Prepare the sauce. Soak the mushrooms in warm water to cover for 5 minutes. (Halve and rinse fresh morels.) Drain the mushrooms, halve them lengthwise and rinse briefly. Cut into small pieces. Heat the butter in a skillet and add the morels and shallots. Cook over low heat until the shallots are tender. Add the cream and simmer, stirring often, until the sauce is lightly thickened, about 15 minutes. Season with salt, white pepper and nutmeg to taste. The sauce can be prepared and gently reheated just before serving.

Rub any fuzz from the fiddlehead ferns and trim the tails to leave about ½ inch. Drop them into boiling salted water and cook until tender, about 5 minutes. Drain well. At serving time, heat them through in the butter.

About 20 minutes before serving time, sprinkle the pheasant breasts lightly with salt and white pepper and let them sit at room temperature until you are ready to cook. Heat the butter in a large, heavy skillet. When it foams, add the breasts and brown lightly for about 5 minutes. Turn and cook over moderately low heat until they are nicely browned and barely done in the center, about 5 more minutes. Remove them and let them sit for 5 minutes.

Drop the noodles into a large quantity of boiling salted water. Return to a boil, stirring. Cook about 1 minute, just until tender. Drain them thoroughly and toss with three-quarters of the sauce.

Arrange the fettuccine on 4 serving plates. Slice each pheasant breast in 6 vertical slices and fan over the pasta. Top with the remaining sauce and surround with the fiddlehead ferns.

At Tapawingo, a country inn/bistro in Ellsworth, Michigan, chef-owner Harlan Peterson makes full use of Michigan's year-round bounty, serving recipes such as this in the pleasant dining room at left.

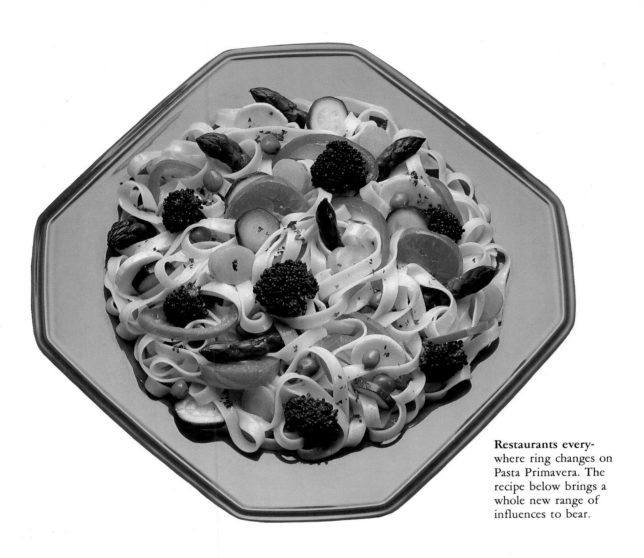

Restaurants everywhere ring changes on Pasta Primavera. The recipe below brings a whole new range of influences to bear.

Buckwheat Pasta with Ham, Kale and Sweet Potatoes

Serves 6

12 tablespoons (6 ounces) butter
2 cups thinly sliced onions
½ cup red wine
2 sweet potatoes, baked, peeled and cubed, about 1 pound
4 cups chopped fresh kale
1 cup slivered country ham (such as Smithfield)
3 cups heavy cream
¼ cup chicken broth
Salt and pepper to taste
1 pound buckwheat pasta

Heat 8 tablespoons (½ cup) of the butter in a large heavy skillet on low heat. Add the onions and cook slowly, about 10 minutes, stirring occasionally, just until they begin to brown. Spoon out or strain the butter from the pan and add the red wine. Cook slowly, until no liquid remains. Remove the onions from the pan and chop them coarsely.

Heat the remaining 4 tablespoons of butter in the skillet and add the chopped onions, the sweet potatoes, kale and the ham. Cook for 2 minutes, stirring occasionally. Add the cream, chicken broth and salt and pepper. Simmer over very low heat, until the sauce thickens.

Cook the buckwheat pasta in a large quantity of boiling salted water just until it is "al dente." Drain thoroughly and toss gently with the sauce.

A luscious combination of fascinating flavors from Anne Rosenzweig, co-owner of Arcadia Restaurant in New York City.

Calzone of Prosciutto, Mozzarella and Ricotta

Makes 6 large turnovers

1 package dry yeast
1¼–1⅓ cups warm water
⅛ teaspoon sugar
4 cups unbleached flour
1 teaspoon salt
½ pound mozzarella cheese, cut into ¼-inch cubes
   (1½ cups)
6 tablespoons finely chopped fresh basil
½ pound thickly sliced prosciutto, cut into ⅛-inch squares
   (about 1¼ cups)
1 cup ricotta cheese
1 egg beaten with 2 tablespoons water

Stir the yeast into ¼ cup of the water. Stir in the sugar and let stand 10 minutes, until foamy. If the mixture does not become fluffy, start again with fresh ingredients.

Combine the flour and salt in a mixing bowl. Make a well in the center of the flour and pour in the dissolved yeast, working the flour into the liquid. Gradually stir in additional water to make a medium-soft dough. Turn onto a floured surface and knead until very smooth and shiny, about 10 minutes.

Place the dough in a floured bowl, cover with a towel and let rise in a warm place until it is at least doubled in bulk, about 1½ hours. Punch down the dough, then knead it briefly on a lightly floured board. Cut it into 6 pieces. Form each into a tight ball, cover with a towel and let them sit for 15 minutes.

Preheat the oven to 400 degrees.

Roll one ball of dough to form a circle about 8 inches in diameter. Toss together the mozzarella and basil and sprinkle 3 tablespoons of this and 3 tablespoons of the prosciutto on half of the circle, leaving a 1-inch margin. Top with 2 tablespoons of the ricotta, in small dollops.

Brush the exposed dough margins with the egg and water mixture. Fold over the dough and press lightly to seal. Fold up and twist this sealed margin to make a decorative edge, pressing to seal tightly. Set the calzone on a non-stick (or lightly oiled) baking sheet. Repeat until you have made 6 calzone, 3 on a sheet. Brush with the egg glaze.

Bake the calzone in the preheated oven until they are lightly browned, about 30 minutes, switching and reversing the pans halfway through baking. Serve warm.

These generously sized turnovers are served at the bright and bustling LaScala Presto Trattoria in Beverly Hills. The crust is firm and crunchy and the filling savory and full-flavored. They would make an ideal light lunch with a salad—or can be eaten out of hand if you can't wait.

Black Bean Ragout with Snails

Serves 4

½ cup dried black beans, soaked overnight in
  cold water to cover
1 ham hock
1½ tablespoons Chinese fermented black beans
1 tablespoon butter
¼ cup julienne of fresh fennel
1 clove garlic, crushed
¼ cup hot salsa
1½ tablespoons red wine vinegar
2–3 tablespoons Bûcheron or Montrachet goat cheese
8 thin slices of French bread, preferably
  the long, thin "ficelle" type
28 cooked snails (available in cans)
¼ cup julienne of peeled, roasted red bell pepper
1 tablespoon chopped fresh cilantro

Drain the beans and put them in a 2-quart saucepan with the ham hock and fermented black beans. Add cold water to cover the ingredients by 2 inches. Bring the water to a boil, skimming off any froth that rises to the surface. Reduce the heat and simmer for 2 to 3 hours, until the beans are tender. Remove and discard the ham hock. Reserve the beans and about 1 cup of the liquid, or enough to give the beans a stewlike consistency.

Preheat the broiler.

Heat the butter in a large skillet. Add the fennel and cook over moderate heat, for about 5 minutes, until tender. Add the beans, the bean liquid, the garlic, salsa and vinegar and stir. Cook over low heat for 20 minutes, stirring occasionally.

Spread the goat cheese on the bread slices. Place under the broiler for 1 to 2 minutes, just until golden.

Taste the beans and adjust the seasonings if needed. Add the snails and cook for 5 minutes, until they are heated through. Remove the beans from the heat and stir in the roasted peppers.

Divide the ragout among 4 serving plates and sprinkle with cilantro. Place 2 cheese-topped croutons at the sides of each plate.

Chef Jimmy Schmidt's inventiveness established his fame at the London Chop House in Detroit. Now he has gone West to establish the Rattlesnake Club in Denver, where he is chef and partner. This recipe shows his innovative approach to food, with influences from Cuba, China, France, Italy and Mexico.

This stunning photograph pays homage to hot peppers and spices by depicting a host of fragrant ethnic morsels from what used to be called the Orient.

Barbecued Duck and Cornmeal Pancakes with Tomato-Chili Salsa

Serves 8–10 as an appetizer
Serves 4 as a main course

Barbecue sauce:

¾ teaspoon salt
¾ teaspoon dry mustard
½ teaspoon finely chopped garlic
1½ bay leaves
½ teaspoon chili powder
⅓ cup Worcestershire sauce
¼ cup cider vinegar
1¾ cups beef or duck broth
3 tablespoons corn oil
¾ cup beer

Duck:

8 duck legs and thighs
2 tablespoons corn oil
3 ears of corn
½ cup finely chopped red bell pepper
½ cup finely chopped green bell pepper
¼ cup finely chopped onion
¼ teaspoon finely chopped garlic
¼ cup chili powder
½ teaspoon salt
¼ teaspoon cayenne pepper
1 egg, beaten
¼ cup stone-ground cornmeal
½ cup Cornmeal Pancake batter,
    page 45

Tomato-Chili Salsa:

2 cups chopped tomatoes
½ cup finely chopped red onion
1 jalapeño pepper, seeded
    and finely chopped
1 red bell pepper, seeded
    and finely chopped
1 green bell pepper, seeded
    and finely chopped
3 tablespoons fresh lime juice
Freshly ground black pepper
2 tablespoons finely chopped cilantro
¼ cup finely chopped Italian parsley

4 Cornmeal Pancakes, page 45

To make the barbecue sauce, combine all the ingredients in a non-corrodible bowl, cover and refrigerate.

To prepare the duck, coat the pieces with about ½ cup of the barbecue sauce and let them marinate for several hours or overnight.

Light a large charcoal fire and let it burn until the coals are covered with gray ash and are very hot. Place the duck on the center of the grill, over the hottest coals, and sear evenly on each side. Baste the meat constantly with the barbecue sauce.

Move the duck to the outer edges of the grill, where the coals are cooler, and cook for 20 to 30 minutes on each side, basting constantly. The meat should be tender and moist.

Remove the duck from the grill and let it cool. When it is cool enough to handle, remove and discard the bones. Chop the meat and skin and place them in a bowl.

Heat the 2 tablespoons of oil in a large skillet. Scrape the corn kernels from the cobs with a sharp knife. Cook the corn, peppers, onion and garlic on low heat for about 10 minutes, stirring frequently. Sprinkle with the chili powder, salt and cayenne, and stir constantly for 2 minutes, to cook the chili powder. Add ¼ cup of barbecue sauce and mix well. Pour the mixture over the chopped duck and toss together.

Combine the egg with the cornmeal and the Cornmeal Pancake batter, and add to the duck mixture. Stir to mix well.

To make the Tomato-Chili Salsa, combine all of the ingredients in a non-corrodible bowl and refrigerate, covered, until serving time. Preheat the oven to 350 degrees.

Lightly butter an 8-inch round cake pan and line it with an 8-inch circle of kitchen parchment. Place 1 cornmeal pancake in the pan, on top of the paper. Spread a ½-inch layer of the duck mixture over the pancake. Repeat until all 4 pancakes are used, ending with a pancake. Top with another round of parchment, then cover the pan with a double layer of aluminum foil, crimping the edges to seal.

Place the cake pan in a roasting pan and pour in about 2 inches of boiling water. Bake in the preheated oven for 35 to 40 minutes. Remove and let cool, covered, for 15 minutes.

Peel the foil and parchment from the top. Run a thin-bladed knife around the inside of the pan and invert the pan onto a cake plate. Peel off the bottom layer of parchment.

Cut into wedges and serve with the Tomato-Chili Salsa.

A dish of contrasting flavors that happily combines spicy barbecued meat with mild-tasting pancakes and a sharp, cool salsa, dreamed up by Larry Forgione, chef-owner of An American Place in New York City. He sometimes substitutes pork for the duck, using 2½ pounds of pork butt, cut into 1-inch-thick steaks.

The heat is on in the kitchen, where the cheerful chef grills a riotous abundance of food into submission and the peppers are hot enough to cry from.

Chili — The Real McCoy

Serves 4–6

4 tablespoons rendered beef fat
  or olive oil
4 cups chopped onion
  (about 2 very large onions)
8 cloves garlic, chopped
4 pounds well-marbled beef chuck,
  trimmed and cut into ½-inch cubes
2 teaspoons salt
2 tablespoons whole cumin seeds
⅓ cup mild, pure chili powder
2 tablespoons Mexican oregano or
  1 tablespoon oregano and
  2 teaspoons marjoram
1–2 teaspoons cayenne pepper
4 cups beef broth
About 1 cup water
2–3 tablespoons yellow cornmeal,
  optional

Heat the beef fat in a large skillet. Add the onions and garlic. Cook over low heat, stirring occasionally, until very tender, but not browned, about 20 minutes.

Meanwhile, place a heavy casserole over moderate heat. Add the beef, toss with the salt, and cook, uncovered, stirring often, until the meat is no longer pink, 10 to 15 minutes.

Toast the cumin seeds in a small heavy skillet, stirring and shaking the pan constantly over moderate heat. After a few minutes the seeds will darken slightly and become extremely fragrant. Let them cool completely before pulverizing to a powder in a spice grinder.

Scrape the onion mixture into the beef. Stir in the ground cumin, chili powder, oregano and cayenne pepper, and continue stirring for 3 to 4 minutes. Add the broth and water and bring to a boil.

Reduce the heat and simmer gently, uncovered, for 1½ hours, adding water if the chili becomes too thick. Taste to adjust the seasonings. Cook another 30 minutes or so, until the meat is tender.

If you like the chili thicker, gradually sprinkle with the cornmeal, stirring constantly. Simmer 5 to 10 minutes longer.

NOTE: Whole cumin seeds, pure chili powder and Mexican oregano are available in many gourmet shops.

A classic Texas chili, simple, tasty and terrific, from Michael McLaughlin, chef/co-owner of Manhattan Chili Parlor in—guess where.

The Commander's Palace Duck Jambalaya

Serves 6

2 ducks
4 tablespoons butter
1 onion, chopped
1 green bell pepper, chopped
3 stalks celery, chopped
5 cloves garlic, finely chopped
3 bay leaves
½ teaspoon thyme
1 tablespoon sweet paprika
35-ounce can tomatoes, chopped
3 cups Duck Stock, page 167
2 tablespoons Louisiana hot sauce
1 tablespoon Worcestershire sauce
Salt
1 bunch scallions, chopped
2 cups converted long grain rice

Skin the ducks. Remove the meat from the bones and cut it into 1½-inch cubes. Set the meat aside and freeze all the bones and trimmings to make duck stock at another time.

Heat the butter in a heavy 3-to 4-quart casserole. When it is foaming, add the vegetables and garlic and cook over moderate heat, stirring often, for 5 minutes.

Add the duck to the vegetables, along with the bay leaves and thyme. Cook over moderate heat, stirring frequently, for 10 minutes. Add the paprika and stir to mix well. Add the tomatoes, duck stock, hot sauce, Worcestershire and salt to taste. Bring the mixture to a boil, then reduce the heat, cover and cook slowly until the duck is tender, about 30 minutes.

Add the scallions and bring the liquid to a boil. Taste for salt. Check that there is enough liquid to cook the rice — you will need about 4 cups. Add more stock or some water, if needed. Stir in the rice and cook, covered, over very low heat, stirring occasionally, for about 30 minutes, or until the rice is tender.

Above, an array of spicy dishes from the kitchen at Carolina, in New York City, features such house specialties as green chili soufflé and gazpacho salad; at right, a little knife work in Stars' kitchen in San Francisco—part of the hours of preparation that precede every good meal.

Chicken with Ancho Chili Sauce

Serves 8 as an appetizer

Annato oil:

1 teaspoon olive oil
8 annato seeds

Ancho Chili Sauce:

8 dried ancho chilies
2 tablespoons olive oil
1 cup chopped onion
1 clove garlic, halved
1 pound fresh tomatoes, chopped,
    or a 14-ounce can tomatoes,
    drained and chopped
1 sprig epazote, optional
½ teaspoon sugar
Salt and freshly ground pepper

½ cup heavy cream
8 Corn Pancakes, page 44
3 cups shredded, cooked chicken
8 tablespoons sour cream
8 sprigs fresh cilantro

To make the annato oil, heat the olive oil and stir in the annato seeds. Steep for 5 minutes, off the heat. Discard the seeds and reserve the oil for the sauce.

To make the Ancho Chili Sauce, wash the chilies in cold water. Break them apart and remove the stems, seeds and ribs. Soak in hot water for 1 hour, or until they are tender. Drain and pat them dry.

Heat the olive oil in a 1½-quart saucepan. Add the onion and garlic and cook over moderate heat, stirring frequently, for about 10 minutes. Stir in the tomatoes and cook for 2 minutes longer. Let the mixture cool slightly.

Put the onion and tomato mixture, the chilies, epazote, annato oil, sugar, and salt and pepper to taste into the container of a food processor. Puree, then rub the sauce through a sieve, pressing hard to extract as much flavor as possible.

Return the sauce to the pan and stir in the cream. Warm over low heat while you make the Corn Pancakes.

Stir the chicken into the Ancho Chili Sauce and heat for a minute or so, just to warm through.

Place 1 pancake on each of 8 plates and spoon the chicken and sauce over them. Garnish each with a tablespoon of sour cream and a cilantro sprig.

NOTE: Annato seeds, ancho chilies and epazote are available in many gourmet shops and Latin American food stores.

What fun this is—a gorgeous, North-of-the-border version of enchiladas from Chef Bruce Auden of Charley's 517 in Houston.

Pork Havana

Serves 4

Pork:

2 limes
½ cup olive oil
6–8 garlic cloves, peeled and bruised
6 peppercorns, bruised
1 bunch fresh cilantro, chopped
1½ pounds boneless pork loin,
   rolled and tied,
   or 2 pork tenderloins, trimmed
Freshly ground pepper
2 tablespoons corn oil

Black bean sauce:

2 tablespoons corn oil
2 slices thick-cut bacon, chopped
1 small red onion, chopped
1 stalk celery, chopped
1 jalapeño pepper, finely chopped
1 cup dried black turtle beans,
   soaked overnight in the refrigerator,
   in water to cover
1½ tablespoons ground cumin
1 quart Chicken Stock, page 166
1 bay leaf
2 teaspoons sherry wine vinegar
Salt and freshly ground black pepper

2 ripe plantains
   (the skins should be black)
½ cup flour
¼ teaspoon salt
⅛ teaspoon freshly ground pepper
⅛ teaspoon cinnamon
2 tablespoons butter
2 tablespoons corn oil

½ cup sour cream
1 lime, quartered
¼ cup thinly sliced red onions

Strings of hot peppers fill fences in New Mexico; in Florida, a chef displays the catch of the day.

To marinate the pork, squeeze the juice from the limes into a non-corrodible bowl just large enough to hold the meat. Chop the lime rinds and add to the bowl, along with the olive oil, garlic, peppercorns and cilantro. Stir to mix, then add the pork and turn to coat it thoroughly. Cover the bowl and refrigerate 12 to 24 hours, turning once or twice.

To make the black bean sauce, heat the corn oil in a heavy saucepan. Add the bacon and cook over moderate heat, stirring often. When the bacon is half cooked, add the onion, celery and pepper. Reduce the heat and cook, stirring occasionally, for about 10 minutes.

Drain the beans and add them to the vegetables and bacon. Sprinkle with the cumin and cook, stirring, for 1 minute. Add the chicken stock and the bay leaf, and bring to a boil. Reduce the heat and simmer, uncovered, until the beans are tender. This can take from 1 to 2 hours. Stir in the vinegar and salt and pepper to taste.

Peel the plantains and cut them, on the extreme bias, into ½-inch-thick slices. Combine the flour, salt, pepper and cinnamon and dust over the slices. Heat the butter and oil in a heavy skillet and fry the plantains over moderate heat until they are tender and nicely browned, about 15 minutes. Drain on paper towels and keep warm.

Remove the pork from the marinade and pat dry. Slice into 4 equal portions and season with pepper. Heat the corn oil in a heavy skillet and, when it is hot, cook the pork for 10 to 15 minutes, turning once. The meat should be pale pink in the center.

Spoon the black bean sauce into 4 deep plates, mashing the beans slightly with the back of the spoon. Arrange the meat and plantain slices alternately over the beans, and garnish with sour cream, lime quarters and red onion slices.

A Cuban influence spices up this sample of chef-owner Norman Van Aken's new American cuisine at Louie's Backyard in Key West, Florida.

Lobster Enchiladas with Salsa Verde

Serves 4 as an appetizer, 2 as a main course
Preheat the oven to 350 degrees

Salsa Verde:

½ pound fresh tomatillos, husked
1 serrano chile, seeds and ribs
    removed, finely chopped
¼ cup chopped onion
1 clove garlic, chopped
½ cup fish-lobster base
    or bottled clam juice
3 tablespoons chopped cilantro
2 teaspoons ground cumin
½ teaspoon sugar
3 tablespoons butter
1 pound cooked lobster meat, shredded
¼ cup sour cream
¼ cup creme fraîche
Salt and white pepper
2 tablespoons corn oil
4 corn tortillas
½ pound Monterey Jack cheese,
    coarsely grated

Garnish:

½ cup chopped tomatoes
¼ cup chopped pitted black
    California olives
¼ cup chopped scallions

Combine all the ingredients for the Salsa Verde in a saucepan, bring them to a boil and reduce the heat. Simmer for about 10 minutes, or until the tomatillos are tender and can be easily pierced with a fork. Transfer the mixture to a blender or food processor and process briefly; the sauce should not be completely smooth. Reserve.

Heat the butter in a skillet and add the lobster. Stir to coat it with the butter. Remove the pan from the heat and stir in the sour cream and crème fraîche. Season to taste with salt and white pepper, and reserve.

Heat the corn oil in a skillet over moderate heat. Cook each tortilla for about 10 seconds on each side, to soften it, then drain on paper towels.

Fill the tortillas with the lobster mixture and ¾ cup of the jack cheese and roll them. Pour a thin layer of the Salsa Verde into a baking dish and place the enchiladas in the dish, seam side down. Add the remaining sauce, top with the remaining cheese, and bake in the preheated oven for about 10 minutes, until the cheese has melted and is just starting to brown.

Serve with bowls of the chopped tomatoes, olives and scallions for the guests to add to their taste.

NOTE: Tomatillos and serrano chilies are available in gourmet shops and Latin American groceries; fish-lobster base is sold, frozen, in gourmet shops. If you have your own full-flavored fish or fish-and-lobster stock on hand, all the better. Bottled clam juice is a reasonable substitute.

When did enchiladas ever taste this *good? Mark Militello, the chef who created these at Café Max in Pompano Beach, likes to go diving for lobsters on his days off, so one way or another you can always depend on finding totally fresh seafood on the Café Max menu.*

Bottling fresh salsa or
serving "lobster" bread
and jambalaya, hot stuff
brings good times.

Peppered Seafood Sausage

Serves 6–8 as an appetizer

1 pound fish fillets such as sole, flounder, salmon or
    whitefish, all one kind or mixed
½ pound cleaned uncooked shrimp and/or scallops
4–6 jalapeño chili peppers, seeded
½ cup packed cilantro leaves
4 large egg whites (½ cup)
1 tablespoon fresh lemon juice
2 teaspoons ground cumin
2 teaspoons salt
¼ teaspoon ground black pepper
5 feet hog casing, in a continuous length, soaked in
    cold water for a few minutes, or 7 5-by-10-inch
    pieces of kitchen parchment

Cut the fish into long strips; the shrimp and scallops can remain whole. Put the seafood, jalapeños and cilantro through the coarse blade of a meat grinder. Combine the ground seafood with the egg whites, lemon juice, cumin, salt and pepper in a large bowl.

Rinse the hog casing in cold water by letting the water run from the tap directly through it. (The casing should not have any holes.) Gather the casing up onto the sauce stuffing funnel attachment on your meat grinder.

Put the seafood mixture back in the grinder and begin to grind it through. When it begins to emerge from the funnel, tie the end of the casing in a knot, leaving 3 inches of it unfilled for expansion room. Grind the mixture out, taking care not to overstuff the length of sausage; it should be about 1 inch wide. If necessary, squeeze it gently with your hands to make this width as you work. Continue with the entire length; you will have about 4 feet of sausage.

Remove the funnel and use your finger to press out the last remaining seafood mixture. Leave 3 inches for expansion and tie the end in a knot. Shape to make it even. Coil it into a spiral and set it aside.

Bring 1 inch of water to a boil in a large heavy skillet with a lid. Reduce the heat so that the water barely quivers. Prick the sausage with a sharp knife point at 3-inch intervals. Place it in the barely moving water, cover the pan and cook for 10 minutes. Turn off the heat and let the sausage rest for 10 minutes before serving.

NOTE: If you use kitchen parchment, butter the paper and place ½ cup of the mixture on each piece. Roll it up, twist the ends and tie them securely with string. Poach as directed.

Chef Michael Roberts of Trumps in Los Angeles sometimes refers to this as "Kickass Sausage," and if you use the full number of jalapeños, it can be peppery indeed. A thoroughly original dish, it has few calories and lots of rewards.

Japanese Chicken Soup

Serves 4

2 thin 6-by-8-inch sheets fresh pasta
12 fresh oba or shiso leaves
3 cups Chicken Stock, page 166
1 chicken breast, boned and skinned
2 scallions, cut diagonally
    into ⅛-inch slices
1 tablespoon grated fresh ginger
2 tablespoons julienned carrot
2 tablespoons julienned turnip
Salt and freshly ground white pepper

Lay 1 sheet of the pasta on a flat work surface and brush off any excess flour it may have accumulated. Brush the sheet lightly, but completely, with cold water. It should be damp and a little sticky, but not wet and soggy.

Cut off the stems of the oba leaves and lay them out on the pasta in 2 rows of 6. Press the leaves lightly into the dough. Lay the second sheet of pasta directly over the first sheet, to sandwich the leaves. Seal the 2 sheets together by pressing firmly with a rolling pin, or by running them through the rollers of a pasta machine at the next-to-thinnest setting. The leaves should show through the thin pasta. Cut the pasta into squares with a knife or pastry cutter so that there is 1 whole leaf contained in each square. The squares should be 2 to 2½ inches on each side.

Bring a large pot of salted water to a rapid boil. Drop in the pasta squares and cook for about 3 minutes, just until "al dente."

Bring the chicken stock to a simmer. Slice the chicken into thin strips and poach in the simmering stock for 5 minutes. Add the scallions, ginger, carrot and turnip and simmer for 2 more minutes. Season with salt and white pepper.

Put 3 of the cooked pasta squares in each of 4 bowls. Pour the broth over the squares and distribute the vegetables and chicken among them. Serve immediately.

NOTE: Oba and shiso are names used interchangeably for a broad, flat green leaf, a distant botanical relative of mint. It is available in Japanese food shops and some Asian groceries.

An exquisite recipe with a strong California influence from Chef Mark Peel of Maxwell's Plum in New York City.

Lobster Braised with Gewürztraminer and Indonesian Spices

Serves 2

2 1½-pound lobsters
1 tablespoon butter
1 cup coarsely chopped leeks
1 cup flour
1 cup dry white wine
1 cup fish-lobster base
   or bottled clam juice
Salt and white pepper

Sauce:

½ cup Gewürztraminer
½ cup heavy cream
⅛ teaspoon mace
⅛ teaspoon ground coriander
¼ teaspoon pulverized lemon grass
⅛ teaspoon ground cumin
⅛ teaspoon pulverized saffron
¼ teaspoon curry powder

Previous page: The staff of Richard King's American Restaurant line up for the camera, framed by the backdrop of Kansas City's Crown Center. Above: The Asian influence is a mighty one, as these recipes and photographs (all of American origin) show. Shape, color and a geometric purity of line are no longer solely the exclusive properties of the mysterious East. These days there is ChiAM, ThaiAM, JapAM and IndoAM.

Bring a very large pot of salted water to a boil. Plunge the lobsters into the pot, cover it and boil them for 6 minutes. Remove the lobsters and cool under cold running water.

Break the lobster claws and carefully remove the meat, in 1 piece if possible. Cut the tail open from the bottom and extract the meat in 1 piece. Cut it in half lengthwise. Reserve the lobster heads for garnish.

Break the lobster shells into small pieces. Melt the butter in a saucepan over moderate heat, add the shells and the cup of chopped leeks, and cook for 5 minutes, stirring frequently. Sprinkle with the flour and cook, stirring, for 2 more minutes. Add the white wine and the fish-lobster base or clam juice. Bring the mixture to a boil, then reduce the heat and simmer for 1 hour, stirring occasionally. Strain through a sieve, pressing down on the shells to extract as much flavor as possible. Discard the solids. You will need ½ cup of the liquid; freeze any excess for future use.

You can refrigerate the lobster and the ½ cup of broth for 24 hours at this point, or continue with the recipe, as you prefer.

Preheat the oven to 350 degrees.

Put the lobster meat into an ovenproof skillet and season with salt and pepper. Pour the Gewürztraminer over the lobster and bake for 8 minutes. Remove the lobster meat and reserve. Add the cream to the skillet, place over moderate heat, and cook until reduced to ⅓ cup. Add the reserved ½ cup of broth and the spices and cook on low heat for 3 minutes.

Add the reserved lobster meat to the sauce and cook just long enough to heat through, about 1 minute.

Set the reserved lobster heads on 2 plates and put the claws at the sides and the tail meat at the bottom. Spoon a little sauce over the lobster and pass the remaining sauce separately.

At Rarities, in the Charles Hotel in Boston, Chef Walter Zuromski serves this subtly and deliciously sauced lobster with a mélange of beautifully cut, color-ful, blanched vegetables which are briefly steamed at serving time: olive-shaped pieces of turnip and zucchini, whole baby leeks, button mushrooms, shelled peas and tomato concasse.

Escargot-Chanterelle Stew

Serves 2

½ pound chanterelles, trimmed
4 tablespoons butter
8 parsley stems, finely chopped
5 scallions, finely chopped
1 clove garlic, finely chopped
16 snails
2 tablespoons flour
2 cups Chicken Stock, page 166
1 cup dry white wine
1 teaspoon basil
2 cloves
1 teaspoon thyme
1 bay leaf
Salt and white pepper
3 egg yolks
1 tablespoon white vinegar
3 tablespoons cream

Slice a few of the chanterelles and cook them in the butter for 5 minutes. Skim the slices from the pan and reserve for garnishing the stew. Add the parsley stems, scallions, garlic, snails and the remaining chanterelles to the butter and cook for 5 minutes. Add the flour and stir until the flour looks gritty. Slowly add the chicken stock, wine, herbs and spices, season to taste, and simmer for 2 hours.

Beat the egg yolks, vinegar and cream together and stir in a little of the simmering liquid. Turn the heat to the lowest point and add the egg yolk mixture to the stew. Stir until creamy and silken. Serve in shallow bowls, garnished with the chanterelle slices.

Two country inn recipes: from the Captain Whidbey Inn (above) in Washington State, and from the Inn at Little Washington, Virginia.

Shiitake Mushrooms with Vermicelli

Serves 8–10 as an appetizer

2½ cups chopped tomatoes
¼ cup tomato paste
1 tablespoon balsamic vinegar
⅓ cup red wine vinegar
2½ teaspoons dried thyme
½ teaspoon herbes de Provence, optional
3 tablespoons sugar
Salt and freshly ground pepper to taste
¼ teaspoon Tabasco sauce
1 cup plus 2 tablespoons olive oil
2 cups thinly sliced onions
2¼ teaspoons finely chopped garlic
1¼ pounds shiitake mushrooms
¼ pound vermicelli or capellini
2 tablespoons finely chopped scallions or chives
1½ teaspoons sesame oil
1 teaspoon soy sauce
¼ teaspoon grated fresh ginger
⅛ teaspoon five-spice powder

Combine the tomatoes, tomato paste, vinegars, thyme, herbes de Provence, if using, sugar, salt, pepper and Tabasco in a non-corrodible saucepan. Bring to a boil, reduce the heat and let the sauce simmer gently.

Heat ¼ cup of the olive oil in a heavy skillet and add the onions. Cook, stirring, until they are wilted and add to the simmering sauce. Let the sauce cook until it is quite thick, about 30 minutes. Stir in 2 teaspoons garlic and remove from the heat.

Remove the shiitake stems and save for future use. Cut the caps into thin slices; there should be about 10 cups.

Heat ¾ cup of the olive oil in a large skillet until very hot. Add half the mushrooms and salt and pepper. Cook, stirring often, until the mushrooms are crisp, about 5 minutes. Drain the mushrooms, but reserve the oil and return it to the skillet to reheat. Add more oil, if needed, and cook the remaining mushrooms until crisp. Season with salt and pepper. Add the drained mushrooms to the tomato sauce and stir to mix well. Let the sauce cool to room temperature.

Bring a large quantity of water to a boil and cook the vermicelli or capellini for about 3 minutes, until just barely tender. Drain the pasta and cool under running water until it is chilled. Drain thoroughly.

Combine the remaining 2 tablespoons of olive oil, the scallions or chives, sesame oil, soy sauce, the remaining ¼ teaspoon of garlic, ginger and spice powder in a large serving bowl. Add the pasta and toss to coat the strands. Divide it among 8 to 10 plates and mound some mushroom sauce neatly in the center of each plate of pasta.

Baked Apples with Wild Mushrooms for James Beard, with American Morel Sauce

Serves 4

American Morel Sauce:

5 tablespoons butter
¼ cup chopped onion
1 carrot, chopped
1 small stalk celery, chopped
2 tablespoons chopped shallots
1 small clove garlic,
   peeled and bruised
Wild mushroom trimmings
   (from following recipe)
1 cup brandy
½ cup port
½ cup dry white vermouth
2 quarts Chicken Stock, page 166
1 ounce dried morels, tied
   in cheesecloth

Baked Apples with Wild Mushrooms:

2 tablespoons butter
½ teaspoon chopped shallots
12 ounces wild mushrooms trimmed
   and cut into ½-inch pieces
Salt
Freshly ground black pepper
1½ cups American Morel Sauce
4 medium-size baking apples
4 cups water
¼ cup white wine
½ cup lemon juice
½ cup Chicken Stock, page 166
¼ cup fresh white breadcrumbs
2 tablespoons chopped parsley

To make the American Morel Sauce, heat 2 tablespoons of the butter in a heavy 4-quart saucepan. Gently cook the onion, carrot, celery, shallots, garlic and wild mushroom trimmings until the onion is transparent but not browned, about 5 minutes. Strain through a sieve to remove excess butter and return the vegetables to the pan.

Add the brandy, port and vermouth to the vegetables and deglaze the pan, over moderate heat, by scraping down the sides and the bottom to loosen any particles. Boil, uncovered, until the liquid is reduced to ¼ cup, about 15 minutes.

Add the stock and the cheesecloth bag of morels. Simmer, uncovered, for 1 hour, or until the liquid is reduced by half. Remove the morels and, when they are cool, slice them.

Strain the reduced sauce through a sieve into a 2-quart saucepan. Add the sliced morels and simmer for 10 minutes. Remove the pan from the heat and measure out 1½ cups of sauce. Reserve the remaining sauce for future use and return the 1½ cups to the pan. Place the pan on very low heat and, little by little, whisk in the remaining 3 tablespoons of butter.

Preheat the oven to 400 degrees.

To make the Baked Apples with Wild Mushrooms, heat the butter in a heavy skillet until it foams. Add the shallots and wild mushrooms and cook gently for 5 minutes, until the shallots are softened. Season lightly with salt and pepper. Spoon out any excess butter and stir in ½ cup of the sauce. Cook, stirring, until the sauce thickens, about 10 minutes. Remove from the heat.

Cut into each apple through the core to make a funnel-shaped indentation. Cut away the pulp to make a larger, conical cup in each apple, leaving a ½- to ¾-inch shell. Combine the water, wine and lemon juice in a large saucepan; add the apples and bring to a boil. Lower the heat and simmer, uncovered, until the apples are poached but still firm, 5 to 10 minutes. Drain thoroughly.

Season each apple with salt and pepper and fill with the mushroom mixture. Place the apples in a roasting pan just large enough to hold them. Add the ½ cup of stock and sprinkle each apple with the breadcrumbs. Bake, uncovered, in the preheated oven until the filling is hot and the breadcrumbs are lightly browned, about 10 minutes.

Warm the remaining cup of sauce and spoon onto 4 plates. Place an apple on each and garnish with the parsley.

A splendid recipe from Larry Forgione, chef-owner of An American Place, one of the trend-setting restaurants of the 1980s. Appropriately, it honors James Beard, beloved mentor of so many of us who like fine food and love to cook. American Bistro owners enjoy describing the elements of their special dishes in the titles—and Larry is no exception.

Veal with Morels, Cranberries and Tarragon Leaves

Serves 2

2 ounces (about 1 cup) fresh morels
   or ¾ ounce dried
4–5 tablespoons butter
½ pound thinly pounded veal scallops,
   preferably cut from the leg
1 tablespoon good wine vinegar,
   such as a Cabernet vinegar
   from California
20 cranberries
⅓ cup red wine
6 fresh tarragon leaves
Salt and freshly ground pepper

If you are using fresh morels, cut them in half lengthwise and rinse them thoroughly under cold running water. Drain and pat them dry with paper towels.

If you are using dried morels, soak them in cold water for 20 minutes. Agitate them to loosen any dirt. Lift them out of the water with a slotted spoon and drain. Cut the morels in half lengthwise and rinse carefully. Drain and pat them dry with paper towels.

Heat 3 tablespoons of the butter in a large skillet over high heat. When the butter begins to brown, add the veal. Cook for 2 to 3 minutes on each side, until lightly browned. Transfer the meat to warmed plates.

Deglaze the pan with the vinegar. Add another tablespoon of butter, if needed, and sauté the morels for 5 minutes. Add the cranberries and the wine and simmer for 3 minutes. Add the tarragon and remove from the heat. Whisk in 1 tablespoon of butter, a little at a time, and season to taste. Spoon the sauce over the veal.

Chef Billy Della Ventura of Chicago's 95th Restaurant here incorporates cranberries in the nouvelle cuisine hierarchy.

Cornucopia

*V*ast, sheer abundance, flowing
onto our tables—foods once deemed exotic
appear in our markets, year round.
The game we once used to hunt
is now raised tame for us to eat.
And we consume kiwi fruit
as if it had journeyed no farther
than from California—which is true.

What once was wild is now tamed. Therefore, what once was sporadic, occasional, surprising has become almost routine. "Taming the truffle" is the current food in-joke. We have marshalled everything else—why not that most vagrant of delicacies, the truffle, a spontaneous act of nature that once only a pig's snout could reliably discern?

We have today not only plenty, but the technology to fiddle with it, so that vegetables, for example, are taking on the most amazing new colors, shapes and sizes. Broccoli, if you can believe it, is going white and blue and purple, whereas formerly we were quite content with green. Oranges now come in close to 20 different forms, and raspberries are available all year long, traveling from as far away as Chile so that we can taste summer on our winter nights.

Our cup literally spilleth over and the least whim of a diner can be answered, in moments, by something fresh on a plate. Side of venison out of season? Flown in, with the gooseberries, from New Zealand. A nasturtium flower to nibble in your salad? The chef will pluck it from his own garden.

In the serendipity of our enlightened national palate, in the seemingly endless pouring forth of provender, we are learning an important lesson about abundance, which is that it is not to be wasted, but rather to be cherished. Strange as it seems, plenty inspires appreciation, particularity, so that today we are making more out of less, much as the Chinese and other nations less prodigal than ourselves have always done. And along with them, we marvel that food, the necessity of life, can be one of the simplest, most subtle rewards in the world.

Squab with Basil and Garlic

Serves 4
Preheat the oven to 450 degrees

4 fresh squab (about 1 pound each),
   with their livers
Salt and freshly ground pepper
4 cloves garlic, peeled and
   lightly crushed
1½ tablespoons clarified butter
1 tablespoon finely chopped shallots
½ cup dry white wine
1½ cups Chicken Stock, page 166
½ cup veal stock, optional
½ cup fresh basil leaves
½ cup heavy cream
1 tablespoon butter

The two quintessential bistros on these pages could not be more different. Quatorze's setting, in Manhattan's meat district, gives it a flavor of Les Halles, and the food supports this pleasant fancy deliciously.

Season the squab with salt and pepper. Skewer 1 squab liver and 1 garlic clove onto each of 4 toothpicks and place inside each bird.

Heat the clarified butter in an ovenproof skillet or heavy roasting pan just large enough to hold the squabs side by side. Sauté the birds, turning with tongs, until golden brown all over, about 5 minutes, then set them breast side up.

Roast the birds for 10 to 12 minutes, just until the breasts are as red as a medium-rare steak. Transfer the squabs to a warm plate.

Pour all but a tablespoon of fat from the pan and cook the shallots over moderate heat for 1 minute. Add the wine and cook on high heat, deglazing the pan, until it is reduced to 2 tablespoons. Add the chicken stock and the optional veal stock; cook on high heat until the mixture is reduced to about ½ cup of syrupy liquid, 5 to 7 minutes.

Remove the toothpicks from the birds and scrape the livers and garlic into a food processor. Add the basil and the reduced stock, and puree. Add the cream and process briefly. Return the sauce to the pan and heat gently, stirring constantly, just to the simmering point, then remove from the heat and whisk in the butter.

Return the squab to the oven briefly to warm them.

To carve the birds, start at the breastbone and cut along the rib cage, running the knife under the breast meat along one side, to loosen it, then continue downward and remove the thigh, with the drumstick attached. Repeat on the other side and proceed with the remaining birds.

To serve, spoon ¼ cup of sauce on each of 4 warm plates. Arrange the squab with the breast halves close together at the top of the plate and the legs, farther apart, pointing outward.

NOTE: Veal stock is available frozen in gourmet shops.

Delicate yet assertive, this is perfect for a romantic bistro-style dinner. Chef Stephen Lyle of Quatorze in New York City likes to serve the squab with Tomatoes Provençale.

Rabbit Stew with Herbed Dumplings

Serves 4–6

2½-pound rabbit, cut into pieces
1 onion, chopped
2 carrots, chopped
2 stalks celery, chopped
1 bay leaf
⅛ teaspoon thyme
⅛ teaspoon savory
8 black peppercorns
6 parsley stems

Vegetables:

½ cup each matchsticks of celery, carrot,
    parsnip, potato, broccoli stems
    and red bell pepper

Sauce:

2 tablespoons butter or lard
2 tablespoons finely chopped onion
1 clove garlic, finely chopped
2 tablespoons flour
3 cups rabbit broth
Salt and freshly ground pepper

Herbed Dumpling batter, page 119

Greens:

2 tablespoons butter
2 tablespoons finely chopped shallots
1 clove garlic, finely chopped
3 cups packed spinach leaves,
    or a mixture such as collard,
    kale and mustard greens

1 tablespoon finely chopped parsley
    or chives

**Freshfields: A Country
Bistro** (right) delivers
just what it promises—
an attractive and
constantly changing
menu in an appealing
village locale.

Place the rabbit in a 2½-quart saucepan with the onion, carrots, celery, bay leaf, thyme, savory, peppercorns and parsley stems. Cover with 4 to 5 cups of cold water, or more if needed, bring to a boil and skim any froth that rises to the surface. Reduce the heat and simmer gently for 1 to 1½ hours, partially covered, until the rabbit is tender. Remove it from the liquid and let cool. Separate the meat from the bones, in pieces as large as possible, and set aside. Return the bones to the pan and simmer, partially covered, for 2 more hours, then strain the broth and measure out 3 cups.

To prepare the vegetables, bring a large pan of salted water to a boil, add the celery and carrot and cook 1 minute. Add the parsnip and potato and cook 1½ minutes. Finally, add the broccoli and red pepper and cook for 30 seconds longer. Drain the vegetables immediately and immerse them in a large pan of ice water, to set the colors. Drain and set aside.

To prepare the sauce and complete the stew, heat the butter or lard in a large, heavy skillet, add the onion and garlic and cook, stirring frequently, until softened. Add the flour and cook, stirring, for 3 minutes. Whisk in the reserved broth and simmer over low heat for 15 minutes, skimming frequently. Season to taste with salt and pepper and stir in the rabbit meat and blanched vegetables.

When the liquid returns to the simmer, drop the Herbed Dumpling batter in by tablespoonfuls, placing them about ½ inch apart. Cover the pan tightly and cook, undisturbed, for 10 to 15 minutes, until the dumplings are firm and dry in the center.

To prepare the greens, heat the butter in a large skillet, stir in the shallots and garlic and cook, stirring, for 2 minutes. Add the greens and cook, stirring, just until the leaves are wilted.

Divide the greens among warm, shallow bowls. Top with the stew and several dumplings. Sprinkle with parsley or chives and serve.

A country-style stew from Freshfields, in West Cornwall, Connecticut, where Chef Steve Mangan has a particular way with game.

Salad of Grilled Duckling and Spiced Pecans

Serves 4

Boned and trimmed breast of 5- to 6-pound duckling
  (about 12 ounces)
¼ cup soy sauce
2 tablespoons honey
1½ tablespoons sesame oil
2 tablespoons dry sherry
2 large garlic cloves, chopped
1 tablespoon grated ginger

Spiced Pecans:

2 tablespoons Worcestershire sauce
1½ teaspoons butter
1½ teaspoons hot chili oil
1 cup pecan halves
¼ teaspoon coarse salt

¼ cup fresh cranberries
¼ cup balsamic vinegar
¼ cup peanut oil
¼ teaspoon salt
Freshly ground pepper
8 cups bite-sized, lightly packed mixed salad greens

Score each piece of the duck breast by making crosswise cuts, ½ inch apart, through the skin and part of the fat. Combine the soy, honey, sesame oil, sherry, garlic and ginger; marinate the duck for 2 hours.

To prepare the pecans, preheat the oven to 350 degrees. Line a baking sheet with kitchen parchment. Combine the Worcestershire, butter and chili oil in a 9-inch skillet over moderate heat. Add the pecans and the salt; stir briefly until the liquid has evaporated. Transfer the nuts to the baking sheet and bake for 12 minutes, until the oily sheen has almost disappeared. Let them cool completely.

Combine the cranberries with water to cover in a small saucepan. Bring the water to a simmer and when the first berry splits its skin, remove from the heat and drain. Cool and reserve the berries.

Heat a heavy skillet and when it is moderately hot, add the duck breasts, skin side down. Cook 4 to 5 minutes, until the fat is almost completely rendered; it will darken and caramelize. Turn the breasts and cook the other side for about 2 minutes, until just medium-rare. Let them rest for 5 to 30 minutes, as convenient. Just before serving, slice in very thin long strips, across the grain, perpendicular to the scoring.

Mix the vinegar, oil, salt and pepper and toss with the greens. Divide the salad among 4 plates and arrange the duck on top. Sprinkle the pecans and cranberries evenly over all and serve at once.

At Jasper's, above, the colorful salad of grilled duckling and spiced pecans is served amid sparkling lights and elegant napery; at the Captain Whidbey, right, you can look up from your duck breast with loganberry sauce and out the window at a sea of fresh green grass.

Steamed and Baked Duck Breast with Loganberry Sauce

Serves 4
Preheat the oven to 450 degrees

Sauce:

½ cup Whidbey's Liqueur (see Note), Chambord or Framboise
⅓ cup brandy
½ cup strained loganberry or raspberry puree
1½ cup rich Duck Stock, page 167
1 teaspoon cold water
1½ teaspoons cornstarch

4 skinless, boneless duck breasts (about 4 ounces each)
Salt and freshly ground pepper
2 tablespoons butter
1 shallot, finely chopped
1½ pounds fresh spinach, washed, stemmed and coarsely chopped

To prepare the sauce, combine the liqueur and brandy in a heavy, non-corrodible saucepan over moderately high heat. Bring to a boil and cook until reduced to about ½ cup. Add the berry puree and simmer until the mixture is reduced to ½ cup, about 3 minutes.

Reduce 1 cup of duck stock to ½ cup, using a separate small saucepan; it will take about 5 minutes. Add it to the berry mixture and bring to a simmer. Combine the water and cornstarch in a bowl and add ½ cup of the hot mixture, stirring constantly.

Pour the sauce back into the pan and simmer, stirring, for 1 minute. Remove from the heat and keep warm on a hot tray or in a hot water bath.

Place the duck breasts in a baking pan and season lightly with salt and pepper. Add the remaining duck stock to the pan and cover it tightly with aluminum foil. Bake the breasts for about 10 minutes; they should remain pink in the center.

Meanwhile, heat the butter in a large skillet. Cook the shallot for about 2 minutes and add the spinach, stirring to coat with the butter. Cook over high heat, just until it is wilted and all the water has evaporated. Season to taste with salt and pepper.

Arrange a bed of spinach on each of 4 warmed plates. Place a whole duck breast on each and cover with ¼ cup of sauce.

NOTE: Whidbey's Liqueur is made from loganberries at a Washington winery and is distributed nationally. It is named for the Captain Whidbey Inn, Coupeville, Washington.

Two interestingly different treatments of the currently fashionable boneless duck breasts. At Jasper's in Boston, chef-owner Jasper White, who has a well-deserved reputation for chic, sleek new American cuisine, pairs them with all-American cranberries and pecans; at the Captain Whidbey Inn in Washington, Chef Lorren Garlichs, who loves to use local ingredients, sauces them with loganberries, rarely, alas, found outside the Pacific Northwest.

Roast Quail Stuffed with Morels with Port Wine Sauce

Serves 4
Preheat the oven to 500 degrees

8 large dried morels
5 tablespoons butter
8 boned quail, each about 3–4 ounces
Salt and freshly ground pepper
1½ cups Chicken or Poultry Stock, page 166
¼ cup port

Place the morels in a small bowl, cover with warm water, and let stand 3 minutes, just until they can be cut. Slice off and discard the tough stem tips, halve each mushroom lengthwise, then rinse them quickly and dry lightly. Heat 2 tablespoons of the butter in a skillet and sauté the morels for a few minutes, until they are soft. Sprinkle the cavities of the birds with salt and pepper and stuff them with morels.

Heat 2 tablespoons of the butter in an ovenproof skillet or heavy roasting pan large enough to hold the quail in one layer. Brown the birds lightly on all sides and transfer the pan to the upper third of the preheated oven. Roast about 4 minutes, or until the juices are medium-rare; the flesh should be a rich pink, not brown or beige.

Reduce the chicken stock to ¼ cup, until it is a glaze. Reduce the port in a small saucepan until about 1½ tablespoons remain. Combine the chicken glaze and the port and bring to a simmer. Remove from the heat and whisk in the remaining butter.

Serve each diner 2 quails, covered with a spoonful or two of sauce.

A simple and very nice dish of quail, as served by Chef John Pawula at Stephanie's restaurant in Peoria, Illinois (above). He has quite a way with game—for another sample, see Morsels of Rabbit, page 79.

Sautéed Breast of Pheasant with Wild Mushrooms

Serves 4

4 pheasants, about 1 pound each
Salt and freshly ground pepper
16 thin asparagus, trimmed to 3-inch tips
1 packed cup kale, torn into 1-inch pieces
1 large ripe tomato, peeled
6 tablespoons butter
2 shallots, finely chopped
1 leek, white part only, thinly sliced
2 large scallions, sliced
8 large shiitake mushrooms, stems removed,
   cut into ¾-inch wedges
1 cup Chicken or Poultry Stock, page 166
¼ cup dry white wine

Disjoint the pheasants and reserve the legs for another use. Bone the breasts and sprinkle lightly with salt and pepper. Reserve the bones, gizzards and wings for Poultry Stock, page 166.

Cook the asparagus for 3 minutes in boiling salted water and transfer to a bowl of ice water. Cook the kale for 2 minutes and drain and chill it in the ice water. Squeeze out the kale and drain both asparagus and kale on paper towels.

Halve the tomato and scoop out and discard the pulp. Cut the shell into thin strips and reserve.

Heat 2 tablespoons of the butter in a heavy skillet and add the pheasant breasts, skin side down; cook 3 to 4 minutes, until crisp and golden. Turn the breasts and cook 3 to 4 minutes more, just until golden but still pink in the center. Transfer the breasts to a plate, cover loosely with foil and keep warm.

Wipe the skillet and add 2 tablespoons of fresh butter. When it is hot, add the shallots, leek, scallions and mushrooms and cook, partially covered, for 3 minutes, stirring once or twice. Add the stock, wine and salt and pepper to taste, and cook for about 5 minutes, until the mushrooms are tender and the liquid is reduced by half.

Heat the remaining butter in a skillet. Add the asparagus and cook just to warm through. Arrange them in a fan to one side of each of 4 warmed plates. Add the kale to the skillet and stir to warm through and gloss with the butter. Divide it among the plates.

Cut the pheasant breasts into thin diagonal slices and place them on the kale. Cover with some of the mushroom mixture.

Toss the tomato strips in the skillet for 30 seconds, just to take off the chill, and arrange a few pieces on each of the plates.

Another recipe from the country bistro, Freshfields, in West Cornwall, Connecticut, this is both colorful and tasty, with a deliciously earthy flavor in the mushroom mélange that accompanies the pheasant on its bed of kale.

Morels and yet more morels—one of the signatures of the new style in cooking because of their heavenly taste and adaptability and new-found availability.

Warm Quail Salad with Honey-Mustard Vinaigrette

Serves 4
Preheat the oven to 400 degrees

Quail:

4 quail, 4–6 ounces each
1 teaspoon finely ground black pepper
½ teaspoon finely ground
  white pepper
½ teaspoon cayenne pepper
4 teaspoons safflower oil
¼ cup finely chopped onion
¼ cup finely chopped celery
¼ cup finely chopped carrot
4 sprigs fresh thyme,
  or ½ teaspoon dried
1 bay leaf
3 cups Chicken Stock, page 166

Salad:

1 small head Boston or bibb lettuce
1 small head radicchio
3 bunches mâche, 2 ounces each
1 small head chicory
1 carrot, peeled
3½-ounce bag enoki mushrooms
2 tablespoons sherry vinegar
¼ teaspoon salt
3 tablespoons peanut oil
2 tablespoons virgin olive oil

Honey-Mustard Vinaigrette:

¼ cup Dijon mustard
3 tablespoons honey
1 teaspoon safflower oil
2 tablespoons finely chopped shallots
¼ cup honey vinegar
  or white wine vinegar

Rinse the quail and pat them dry. Combine the peppers in a small dish. Using ½ teaspoon for each bird, sprinkle them inside and out with the mixture. Place 3 teaspoons of the oil in a heavy non-corrodible pan over moderately high heat. Add the quail and sear until golden brown, about 2 minutes on each side. Place the pan in the oven and roast the birds for 6 to 8 minutes, until cooked to medium-rare or medium-well done. Remove from the oven and transfer the birds to a plate.

Add the remaining teaspoon of oil to the quail drippings and return the pan to direct heat. Add the onion, celery and carrot and cook on low heat for about 10 minutes, stirring occasionally.

Disjoint the quail. Remove the legs, with thighs attached, and carve the breast meat from the bones in 2 halves, with skin attached. Cover the quail with foil.

Add the quail carcasses to the cooked vegetables, along with the thyme, bay leaf and chicken stock. Bring the mixture to a boil, reduce the heat and simmer, partially covered, for 30 minutes. Strain, discarding the solids. There will be about 2 cups of rich quail stock. Reduce the stock over moderately high heat until it is syrupy and about ⅔ cup of liquid remains. This will take about 8 to 10 minutes. Watch and measure carefully. Reserve the stock.

To prepare the salad, tear the lettuce into bite-sized pieces. Cut the radicchio into thin strips. Pick over the mâche. Discard the dark green leaves from the chicory and use only the pale yellow ones. Cut the carrot into fine, 2-inch-long julienne. Cut off most of the stems from the enoki, leaving about 1 inch attached to the caps.

Combine the sherry vinegar and salt in a small bowl and stir in the peanut and olive oils. Toss with the salad just before serving.

The recipe can be prepared ahead to this point.

To make the Honey-Mustard Vinaigrette, whisk the mustard and honey together in a small bowl. Combine the safflower oil and shallots in a heavy small non-corrodible saucepan and cook over moderate heat for 2 minutes. Add the honey vinegar, bring to a boil and cook until the vinegar has evaporated, about 2 minutes. Stir in the reserved ⅔ cup of quail stock. Bring to a simmer and stir in the honey-mustard mixture. Remove from the heat, but keep warm.

Warm the foil-wrapped birds in a 350-degree oven for a few moments, just to heat through. Cut the breast meat into thin strips.

Toss the salad with its dressing and divide among 4 plates. Arrange the breast meat over the salad. Crisscross a pair of quail legs at the top of the plate and spoon about ¼ cup of the vinaigrette over all. Serve at once.

From Chef Dean Fearing of The Mansion on Turtle Creek in Dallas. The flavors of this elegant, colorful salad are wonderfully complicated, and you will need 3 cups of good homemade stock to do this recipe justice. Fortunately, although time-consuming to prepare, it can be at least partially made ahead—and without question, it is well worth all the effort.

Morsels of Rabbit with Basil and Mustard Sauce

Serves 4

2½-pound fryer rabbit, boned
Salt and freshly ground pepper
4 tablespoons butter
½ cup dry white wine
½ cup heavy cream
1 tablespoon coarse-grained mustard
1 tablespoon Pesto, page 168

Remove any pieces of tendon or membrane on the rabbit. Slice the loin in crosswise slices, ¼ to ½ inch thick, and the leg and thigh sections into strips about ¼ inch wide and 1 inch long. Season lightly with salt and pepper.

Heat the butter in a heavy skillet and when it begins to foam, add the rabbit pieces. Toss until the meat turns white throughout, about 4 minutes. Transfer the rabbit to a plate, using a slotted spoon.

Add the wine to the skillet and cook, stirring constantly, until it is reduced to about 2 tablespoons. Add any rabbit juices that have accumulated on the plate and pour in the cream. Cook over moderate heat until the mixture has thickened somewhat. Remove the pan from the heat and whisk in the mustard and the Pesto. Add the rabbit pieces and return the pan to the heat, just long enough to warm the rabbit. Serve with buttered noodles.

Quail, so beautiful in life, are deliciously tender to eat and a constant inspiration to chefs. Dean Fearing, above, serves the salad opposite in the Turtle Creek dining room.

79

Above, the staircase at Frog in central Philadelphia: a high-tech approach is highlighted by blue neon beneath the overhang. At right, slices of turkey ballotine look simply splendid with a garnish of colorful leaves and berries to complement a striking platter cooked up by Kathy Pavletich Casey of Fullers in Seattle.

Turkey Ballotine with Spicy Sausage Stuffing and Orange Port Sauce

Serves 8–10

½ cup hazelnuts
⅓ cup orange juice
2 tablespoons butter
½ medium-size onion, finely chopped
2 cloves garlic, finely chopped
¾ cup finely chopped celery
1 cup chopped mushrooms
1 whole turkey breast, 5½–6½ pounds
½ pound hot, spicy Italian sausage
1 teaspoon dried sage
¼ teaspoon ground allspice
¼ teaspoon ground cloves
½ teaspoon ground white pepper
½ teaspoon ground black pepper
½ teaspoon poultry seasoning
1–1½ teaspoons salt
1 tablespoon port
2 tablespoons orange liqueur, such as
   Mandarin Napoleon, Grand Marnier
   or Triple Sec
1 egg
¼ cup heavy cream
1½ cups stale bread cubes
1 tangerine, peeled, sectioned,
   seeds removed

Sauce:

2 cups Turkey Stock, page 166
1 shallot, finely chopped
1 clove garlic, finely chopped
⅓ cup port
2 tablespoons orange liqueur
2 tablespoons butter, softened
2 tablespoons flour
2 cups heavy cream
Salt and white pepper

Soak the hazelnuts in the orange juice overnight in the refrigerator.

Chill the bowl and blade of a food processor in the refrigerator.

Heat the butter in a skillet and cook the onion, garlic and celery until the onion is soft and transparent, about 5 minutes. Add the mushrooms and cook, stirring occasionally, for 5 more minutes. Let the mixture cool completely.

Carefully cut away the bones from the turkey breast and reserve them for making stock. Leave the skin intact. Cut away the tenderloins—the long thin fillets on each side—and reserve them. Slicing away from the center, parallel to the work surface, cut the thickest part of the breast to within 1 inch of the sides. Open up the breast to make a large fillet. Cover and refrigerate the turkey.

Remove the long white sinews from the reserved tenderloins and cut the meat into ¾-inch pieces. Process the turkey pieces in the chilled processor until they are finely chopped. Add the sausage meat, sage, allspice, cloves, white and black pepper, the poultry seasoning and salt to taste. With the machine running, slowly add the port, orange liqueur, the egg and the cream. Transfer the mixture to a large bowl.

Drain the hazelnuts, reserving the orange juice. Chop the nuts coarsely and add them to the spiced meat mixture. Add the onion and mushroom mixture and the bread cubes and mix thoroughly. Chill the stuffing. The recipe can be made up to a day ahead to this point.

Preheat the oven to 350 degrees.

Place the turkey breast, skin side down, on a flat surface. Put the stuffing in the center of the meat and distribute the tangerine segments evenly throughout the stuffing. Roll up the turkey, enclosing the stuffing. The meat should overlap slightly. Wrap the roll with butcher twine, making sure the ends are secure. (If there is extra stuffing, bake it separately for 30 to 40 minutes.)

Place the turkey, seam side up, on a rack in a roasting pan. Roast for 1 hour, then turn it to the other side. Roast for an additional 1½ to 2 hours, until the internal temperature registers 140 degrees on a meat thermometer.

To prepare the sauce, cook the turkey stock over high heat until it is reduced to 1 cup. Add the shallot, garlic, port, orange liqueur and reserved orange juice. Bring the mixture to a boil, reduce the heat and simmer for 5 minutes. Mash the butter and flour together in a small bowl and whisk it into the simmering liquid, a little at a time. Simmer for another 5 minutes. Add the cream and bring to a boil. Reduce the heat and simmer, stirring occasionally, until the sauce is reduced and thick enough to coat the back of a spoon. Season to taste with salt and pepper.

Let the ballotine cool for 20 minutes before slicing. Serve on warm plates with the sauce.

Grilled Wild Turkey Breast

Serves 4

1 boned wild turkey breast, split,
   with skin attached (about 1½ pounds
   total from a 6- to 8-pound bird)
1 cup dry white wine
1½ cups cider vinegar
2 cups applejack brandy
¼ cup sugar
2 teaspoons coarsely ground
   black pepper
2 tablespoons mustard seeds
16 sprigs fresh thyme
8 sprigs fresh rosemary
6 sprigs fresh sage
2 tablespoons coarsely chopped garlic
½ cup peanut oil
1 teaspoon coarse salt
1 tablespoon vegetable oil, for oven
   roasting
6 thick slices bacon, halved

Mustard Thyme Butter, page 167

Pristine, fresh
ingredients (above) are
essential for all good
recipes; so are chefs
such as Bradley Ogden
and Michael McCarty,
who value quality
above all else.

The turkey marinates for 2 days before cooking. Be sure to save the bones and carcass for stock.

Combine the wine, vinegar, 1½ cups of the applejack, the sugar, pepper and mustard seeds in a non-corrodible saucepan and place over high heat. Bring to a boil and cook until the mixture has reduced by half, about 15 minutes. Set aside to cool to room temperature.

Fit the turkey breast snugly in a non-corrodible dish. Reserve 4 sprigs of the thyme and add all the herbs, the garlic, peanut oil and salt to the marinade and pour it over the turkey. Cover with plastic wrap and refrigerate for 2 days, turning the turkey twice a day.

Preheat the oven to 325 degrees or prepare a charcoal fire; burn the coals until gray ash appears.

Remove the breast halves from the marinade and pat them dry. Rub lightly with oil and sprinkle with salt and pepper. Strain the marinade, discarding the solids. Add the remaining ½ cup applejack to the liquid to make a basting sauce.

If you are cooking in the oven, place a large, heavy ovenproof skillet over very high heat. Add the tablespoon of vegetable oil and and, when it is almost smoking, add the turkey and sear for about 2 minutes. Turn and sear the other side. Place the skillet in the oven and cook, basting 2 or 3 times, for about 30 minutes, until the internal temperature reaches 160 degrees. Remove the skillet from the oven, cover loosely and let the meat rest for 10 minutes.

If you are grilling, cook over low heat until the turkey is seared on one side. Do not allow the flame to flare. Turn the breasts to the other side and grill, basting and turning frequently, about 30 minutes. Remove from the fire, cover loosely and let the meat rest for 10 minutes.

While the turkey is cooking, cook the bacon until it is crisp but moist, 8 to 10 minutes. Drain on paper towels.

Cut the turkey slightly on the diagonal into ¼-inch slices. Divide among 4 warmed dinner plates, overlapping the slices. Add 3 pieces of bacon to each plate and top with a teaspoon of Mustard Thyme Butter and a sprig of fresh thyme.

A recipe from Bradley Ogden (at right), chef of the Campton Place Restaurant in the Campton Place Hotel, San Francisco. Like many of the outstanding new American chefs, Ogden has sought out the best products from all over the country; hams are cured in Missouri, for example, mushrooms come from Oregon and he grows some of his produce in his own garden.

Salade Pigeon

Serves 2

Raspberry vinegar sauce:

1 cup raspberry vinegar
3 tablespoons finely chopped shallots
1½ cups Chicken or Poultry Stock,
   page 166
1 cup heavy cream
Salt and freshly ground pepper

Salad:

2 pigeons or squabs
10 spinach leaves
2 palmfuls frise (French chicory)
2 walnuts, chopped
10 raspberries

To make the sauce, combine the vinegar and shallots in a non-corrodible saucepan and cook over high heat until reduced to 3 tablespoons of liquid. Add the stock and cook down to about ½ cup of liquid. Add the cream and continue cooking, on high heat, until there is between ½ and ¾ cup of liquid that is sufficiently thickened to coat the back of a spoon and quite concentrated in flavor. Season to taste with salt and pepper.

To make the salad, halve the pigeons and bone them. Grill the birds until medium-rare, about 8 minutes on each side. Let them rest for 10 minutes, then separate the wings and legs and carve the breasts across into thin slices.

Place the spinach on 2 plates in a 5-point star arrangement. Put a palmful of frise in the center of each plate and sprinkle with the walnuts.

Place the raspberries between the spinach leaves at the rim of the plate.

Drape the pigeon breast over the frise and place the wings at the sides and the legs at the base of the plates.

Pour ¼ cup of the sauce over each salad in a circular motion, starting at the center and working outward.

This comes from Michael McCarty (below), of Michael's in Santa Monica, where it is served tepid—not hot and not quite at room temperature.

Foods from the Waters

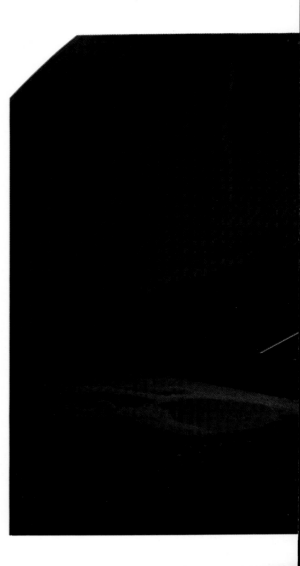

e used to take the sea as we found
it, reaping its rich bounty to serve
at our tables. Today we are seeding
the earth's waters to enhance
the drama and delight of our dining.

The fishermen who must brave the merciless waves to haul in
their catches are probably the last true hunters left in America.
They never know when they set out whether they will bring
back enough to have made their trip worthwhile—and indeed,
they risk not returning at all. It is amazing to realize to what
extent we have managed to domesticate or at least control the
breeding habits of almost everything else we eat. And, although
few people yet realize aquaculture's vast potential, we are now
farming the waters as well.

The artificial hatching of trout and salmon is nothing new;
now we are breeding shrimp and crayfish, too, cultivating them
in what were formerly irrigation ditches for rice paddies in
Tennessee and South Carolina. We are seeding mussels on the
legs of oil-drilling rigs in the Gulf of Mexico, where the
mollusks can grow plump in the warm waters eddying around
the equipment.

And all this activity goes on so that we can occupy a front-
row seat before a display that would have exceeded our parents'
wildest fantasies. Imagine observing a leopard shark sharing
space with the more-familiar mussels, crawfish, catfish and
salmon, as well as specialties you might once have scorned, but
no longer—like monkfish and squid. Set upon a breakwater of
snowy-white ice, they have become part of the décor, serving as
a frosty buffer between the diners on one side and the kitchen
on the other.

Thanks to all this activity, the catch of the day—whether
unloaded from trawlers at the dock, purchased at daybreak at
the wholesale fish market, or flown in packaged in cryovac or
dry ice—now occupies prime space on bistro menus, scrawled in
chalk on a slate or recited by a grinning waitperson, in every
city boasting a waterfront view and a refrigerator in tiptop
condition. America today is a fish-lover's paradise.

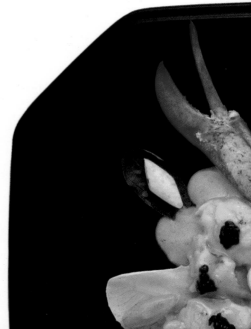

Chesapeake fishermen dredge up oysters, top; left, plastic-covered irrigation ditches become shrimp runs in Tennessee; above, a whole leopard shark at San Francisco's Stars; bottom, lobster blanquette at Déjà-Vu in Philadelphia.

Cassoulet of Mussels

Serves 6

1 pound white Great Northern beans
5 dozen mussels
1 cup white wine
1 cup water
1 medium-size yellow onion, chopped
1 cup finely chopped celery
½ cup finely chopped carrots
3 tablespoons vegetable oil
1 clove garlic, finely chopped
2 small white onions, finely chopped
2 shallots, finely chopped
2 slices bacon, chopped and blanched
   in boiling water for 2 minutes
2 ounces (½ cup) prosciutto,
   finely chopped
2 ripe tomatoes, seeded and chopped
½ cup fine fresh breadcrumbs

Mussels scraped from the rocky ocean margins, deep-water fish in their myriads— the sea's bounty is an almost infinite resource for such kitchen wits as Billy Della Ventura, below with Christian De Vos, manager of Chicago's 95th.

Rinse the beans and soak for 14 hours in sufficient cold water to cover.

Scrub the mussels and remove their beards. Pour the wine and water into a large saucepan. Add the mussels, the chopped yellow onion, and half the chopped celery and carrots. Cover and cook over moderately high heat for 5 minutes, until the mussels have opened. Remove them from the broth and, when cool enough to handle, shell them and refrigerate until needed. Reserve 12 half shells for garnish and discard the rest. Strain the mussel broth through a triple thickness of cheesecloth and discard the solids.

Heat the oil in a heavy skillet over moderately high heat. Cook the remaining celery and carrots, the garlic, white onions and shallots for about 3 minutes, stirring occasionally, until softened.

Drain the beans and put them in a large casserole. Add the strained mussel broth and sufficient cold water to barely cover the beans. Add the cooked vegetables, bacon, prosciutto and tomatoes and stir. Bring to a boil, reduce the heat, partially cover the casserole and simmer gently for about 1½ hours, until the beans are tender. If the beans are refrigerated at this point, allow an extra 15 minutes in the final cooking.

Forty minutes before serving time, heat the oven to 350 degrees. Reserve 6 of the mussels and bury the remainder among the beans. Sprinkle the surface with the breadcrumbs. Bake for 20 minutes. Place the reserved mussels on top, arrange the reserved shells around the edges and bake for 5 more minutes.

This cassoulet, invented and served by Michael Foley at Printer's Row in Chicago, is one of the truly great recipes. If you question the wisdom of adding an onion and shallots, and of using both bacon and prosciutto, never fear. The flavor is incomparable and worth every minute of the fairly considerable preparation time. The entire dish can be assembled in advance and needs only a last-minute reheating — think of it for your next party.

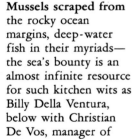

Bluefish Fillets with Red Onion Sauté

Serves 4
Preheat the oven to 400 degrees

Sauce:

2 cups Cabernet Sauvignon or
    other full-bodied red wine
¼ cup sherry wine vinegar
½ cup finely chopped shallots
3 tablespoons heavy cream
½ pound chilled butter,
    cut into 24 pieces
¼ teaspoon sugar
Salt and freshly ground pepper

Onions:

1½ tablespoons butter
2 teaspoons vegetable oil
1½ cups thinly sliced red onion rings
¾ teaspoon sugar
½ teaspoon salt
½ teaspoon red wine vinegar

Fish:

4 bluefish fillets, about 6 ounces each
Salt
1 teaspoon lemon pepper
2 tablespoons butter, melted
1 tablespoon chopped fresh thyme

To make the sauce, combine the wine, vinegar and shallots in a heavy non-corrodible saucepan and cook over moderate heat until the liquid barely covers the shallots, about 30 minutes. Add the cream and cook until the liquid looks thick and shiny, about 5 more minutes. Proceed to beat in the butter, as in Beurre Blanc, page 168. Season with the sugar and salt and pepper to taste.

To prepare the onions, heat the butter and oil in a skillet. When they are hot, add the onions and cook over moderate heat, stirring frequently, until they are soft and translucent, but not brown, about 10 minutes. Stir in the sugar, salt and vinegar and remove from the heat.

To cook the fish, season the fillets with salt and lemon pepper and brush with the butter. Bake in the oven for 8 to 10 minutes, just until the fish starts to flake. Transfer the fillets to 4 warmed serving plates. Strain the sauce over them and garnish with the red onions and the thyme.

At Fedora Cafe & Bar in Kansas City, this is a favorite way of serving sea bass, tuna and swordfish, as well as bluefish, accompanied by steamed new red potatoes in their skins and a lemon half wrapped in cheesecloth and tied with a jaunty bow.

Sautéed Shrimp in Fennel Butter with Shrimp Fritters

Serves 6

Fennel Butter:

1 cup dry white wine
2 shallots, chopped
2 cloves garlic, chopped
1 teaspoon black peppercorns, bruised
8 tablespoons butter, at room
    temperature
1 tablespoon Pernod
1 teaspoon ground fennel
½ teaspoon coarse salt
⅛ teaspoon Worcestershire sauce

Shrimp Fritters:

1½ cups flour
2 teaspoons paprika
1 teaspoon coarse salt
1 teaspoon ground ginger
1 teaspoon sugar
1½ cups beer
Juice of 1 lemon
16 medium-size shrimp, shelled,
    deveined and cut into ¼-inch pieces
¼ cup grated carrots
Vegetable oil for deep-frying

Shrimp:

8 tablespoons butter
30 super-colossal shrimp
    (10 per pound), peeled, deveined
    and butterflied
¾ cup Pernod
Juice of 3 lemons
Salt and freshly ground pepper

Top: Ring changes on the fritters by using the shrimp, carrots and seasonings minus the flour, beer and lemon, and wrapping in egg-roll skins or pasta dough. At right, fresh flowers in the prototypical American bistro, Chez Panisse.

To make the Fennel Butter, combine the wine, shallots, garlic and peppercorns in a small stainless steel or enamel saucepan. Bring to a boil, reduce the heat and simmer for about 25 minutes, until the liquid is reduced to 3 or 4 tablespoons. Let it cool to room temperature and strain. Beat it into the butter with the Pernod, ground fennel, salt and Worcestershire sauce. Chill the mixture until firm.

To make the Shrimp Fritters, combine the flour, paprika, salt, ginger and sugar in a bowl and mix well. Stir in the beer and lemon juice. Fold in the shrimp and carrots.

Heat the oil in a deep-fryer to 360 degrees. Drop ⅛ cup of batter for each fritter into the hot oil and fry until puffed and golden brown, about 5 minutes. Check one from each batch to see that they are done. Drain on paper towels and keep warm in the oven.

Heat the butter in a large skillet. Add 10 to 15 of the shrimp to the pan and sauté for 3 to 4 minutes, or until the shrimp turn pink. Do not crowd the shrimp; cook them in 2 or more batches. Transfer them to a plate as they finish cooking.

Add the Pernod and lemon juice to the juices in the pan and cook over high heat for 3 minutes. Reduce the heat and slowly beat in the Fennel Butter, a little at a time. Return the shrimp to the pan for a minute or two, just long enough to warm through. Season with salt and pepper.

Divide the shrimp among 6 warm plates. Arrange 3 fritters on each and cover with the remaining sauce.

As American—and as buttery—as you can get, from Chef Kenneth Dunn at Richard King's American Restaurant, Kansas City, Missouri.

Grilled Monkfish with Braised Cabbage, Tomatoes and Bacon

Serves 8
Prepare a charcoal fire
*   and preheat the oven to 250 degrees*

4 pounds monkfish, cut into 8 pieces
Salt and freshly ground pepper
¾ cup olive oil
¼ cup fresh lemon juice
1 head green cabbage (about 3 pounds)
1 pound slab bacon
1 cup dry white wine
1 cup fish broth or bottled clam juice
1 cup chopped red onion
2 cups peeled, seeded and chopped
    fresh tomatoes
4 lemons, halved
1 bunch watercress

Trim the monkfish and season it with salt and pepper. Coat the fish with olive oil and lemon juice and refrigerate, covered, until shortly before serving time.

Trim the cabbage and cut out the hard core. Cut it into quarters and cut into ¼-inch-thick slices.

Remove the rind from the bacon and cut it into ½-inch cubes. Place the bacon in 1 or 2 baking pans; it should be well spread out, not crowded. Cook in the preheated oven for 25 minutes. Remove the bacon with a slotted spoon and drain on paper towels.

Heat the wine and fish broth in a large pan. Add the cabbage, the cooked bacon, red onion and tomatoes. Cook, covered, over moderate heat, stirring occasionally, until the cabbage is tender but still crisp, about 20 minutes.

About 10 minutes before the cabbage is ready, grill the monkfish over a medium-hot charcoal fire or cook it under the broiler, allowing 10 minutes of cooking time for each inch of thickness.

Divide the cabbage mixture among 8 warmed deep plates and place the monkfish pieces on top. Garnish each serving with a lemon half and a spray of watercress.

A modern version of a traditional garbure, homey, good-looking and well-flavored, from The Trellis, in Williamsburg, Virginia.

Brook Trout with Vegetable Julienne and Citrus Butter

Serves 4
Preheat the oven to 450 degrees

1 red bell pepper, cut into fine julienne
1 carrot, cut into fine julienne
1 leek, white part only, cut into fine julienne
1 bunch chives, cut into 2-inch pieces
4 whole boneless brook trout, about 10 ounces each
Salt and freshly ground pepper
2 cups dry white wine, at room temperature
2 shallots, finely chopped
2 tablespoons fresh lemon juice
½ pound chilled butter, cut into 24 pieces
1 orange, rind and pith removed, cut into half-circles
1 grapefruit, rind and pith removed, cut into half-circles

Bring a large pan of salted water to a boil and blanch the pepper, carrot, leek and chives for 30 seconds. Drain, plunge them into ice water, then drain again.

Open the trout and sprinkle with salt and pepper. Divide the blanched vegetables among the cavities of the fish and wrap the flaps firmly around the vegetables. Place the fish, belly side down, in a non-corrodible ovenproof skillet. Pour in the wine to reach about one-third of the way up the sides of the fish. Poach in the oven for about 10 minutes, until the fish is just cooked through. Gently transfer the trout to 4 warm plates and keep warm.

Add the shallots and lemon juice to the poaching liquid and place the pan over high heat. Boil rapidly, stirring occasionally, until the liquid has reduced to about 2 tablespoons. Incorporate the butter into the liquid to make a Beurre Blanc, page 168.

Slit the skin down the back of each trout and pull the skin gently away from the flesh. Spoon the sauce over and around the fish and garnish with the orange and grapefruit slices.

A spectacular presentation from Chef Jay Silver at Lavin's Restaurant in Manhattan, which retains the fresh flavors of the fish and crisp, clean texture of the vegetable julienne. The unusual cooking technique, a simultaneous poach and bake at high temperature, sets the flesh to a tender consistency perfectly complemented by the sauce. Each whole, boned fish is set on the plate as if innocently swimming in the pale sauce.

An ethereal treatment of fillets of sole, an earthy seafood stew, and far right, Richard Lavin, whose restaurant specializes in matching food and wine superbly.

Steamed Fillet of Sole with Saffron and Green Peppercorns

Serves 2

1 tablespoon butter
1 shallot, finely chopped
¼ cup dry white wine
1 teaspoon canned green peppercorns, drained and crushed
¾ cup heavy cream
1 teaspoon pulverized saffron
Salt
2 fillets of sole, about 6 ounces each
Freshly ground pepper
8 thin asparagus spears
⅓ cup freshly shelled peas

Heat the butter in a small, non-corrodible saucepan. Cook the shallot for about 2 minutes, until softened. Add the wine and peppercorns and cook on high heat until 2 tablespoons of liquid remain. Add the cream and saffron and cook until the mixture is reduced by half, and is thick enough to coat a spoon. Salt the sauce to taste and keep warm.

Sprinkle the sole lightly with salt and pepper and wrap it in aluminum foil with the asparagus and peas. Steam for 15 to 20 minutes just until the fish starts to flake.

Spoon the sauce onto 2 warmed plates. Place the sole in the center and the peas and asparagus on either side.

An exquisitely simple dish from Chef Billy Della Ventura, of the 95th Restaurant, at the top of the Hancock Building in Chicago. The combination of white and green is particularly pleasing.

Striped Bass in Tomato-Basil Sauce

Serves 6

3 ½-pound whole striped bass
4 medium-size tomatoes
2 garlic cloves, peeled
1 scallion, sliced
1 stalk celery, sliced
1 carrot, sliced
1 bay leaf
2 quarts water
2 tablespoons flour
3 tablespoons olive oil
⅓ cup dry white wine
¼ cup brandy
1 tablespoon Worcestershire sauce
8 tablespoons butter
3 tablespoons finely chopped fresh basil,
 preferably lemon basil
Salt and freshly ground pepper

Cut the head, the narrow tail part and the fins from the fish and reserve. Cut the fish crosswise into 6 steaks of equal weight and refrigerate.

Coarsely chop 2 of the tomatoes and put them in a non-corrodible saucepan. Add the fish trimmings, 1 clove of garlic, the scallion, celery, carrot, bay leaf and the 2 quarts of water. Simmer gently for 1 hour, uncovered, skimming occasionally. Strain the broth. Rinse the pan, return the broth to it, and simmer until it is reduced to 1½ cups.

Peel, seed and chop the remaining tomatoes and reserve. Chop the remaining garlic clove finely. Dredge the fish in the flour. Heat the oil in a large skillet over moderate heat and add the garlic. Add the fish and cook for 2 minutes or so on each side, until not quite cooked. Add the wine and the brandy and light the alcohol. Shake the pan gently until the flames die out. Transfer the fish to a plate and place in a warm oven.

Pour the fish stock into the skillet. Add the Worcestershire sauce, the reserved tomatoes and the butter. Stir over moderate heat until the sauce has thickened slightly and reduced to about 1¼ cups. Stir in the basil and remove from the heat. Add the salt and pepper to taste.

Spoon about 3 tablespoons of sauce onto each plate and set the fish on top of it. Serve at once.

You might want to have the fish filleted prior to cutting it into steaks, but it is less succulent if the bones are removed. It also takes only half as long to cook. The recipe is from Chef Piero Selvaggi of Primi Un Ristorante in Los Angeles, a perfect spot for people who enjoy grazing Hollywood-style—joining the rich and soon-to-be-famous in sampling daisy-shaped pasta stuffed with radicchio and similarly whimsical offerings.

Halibut with Ginger-Lime Butter

Serves 4

¾ cup dry white wine
1 cup water
2 tablespoons fresh lemon juice
Salt
1½ pounds boned and skinned halibut, in 4 fillets
1 tablespoon finely chopped red pickled ginger (beni shoga)
¼ cup rice wine (sake)
2 tablespoons rice vinegar
2 tablespoons fresh orange juice
2 tablespoons fresh lime juice
1 tablespoon finely chopped shallot
1 teaspoon finely chopped garlic
1 teaspoon finely chopped cilantro
½ pound chilled butter, cut into 24 pieces
White pepper
1 orange, rind and pith removed, cut into half-circles
8 sprigs cilantro
12 long thin slices red pickled ginger, rolled into "flowers"
8 sprigs cilantro
1 scallion, green part only, in thin diagonal slices

A feature of the new cooking: fish of all kinds of shapes and sizes, whipped freshly from the water to await their apotheosis at the magic hands of the chef.

Combine the wine, water, lemon juice and ¼ teaspoon of salt in a wide non-corrodible skillet. Bring the liquid to a simmer and add the fish; poach over very low heat until not quite cooked through, about 4 minutes. Set aside.

Combine the chopped ginger, rice wine, vinegar, orange and lime juices, shallot, garlic and chopped cilantro in a heavy non-corrodible saucepan. Simmer, stirring occasionally, until the liquid has reduced to about 1½ tablespoons. Incorporate the butter into it to make a Beurre Blanc, page 168, and season with white pepper.

Strain half the sauce onto 4 warm serving plates. Drain the halibut fillets and pat them dry. Place them on the plates, and strain the remaining sauce over the top. Garnish with the orange slices, ginger and cilantro sprigs. Sprinkle with the scallion and serve immediately.

NOTE: Pickled ginger and rice vinegar are available in Japanese or Asian markets and some gourmet shops.

A creation of Kathy Pavletich Casey, chef of Fullers in the Seattle Sheraton, this elegant dish underscores the traditional French beurre blanc, a creamy suspension, with a combination of Asian influences: zippy pickled ginger, tart rice vinegar and citrus juices, and a hint of garlic and cilantro. Its success depends on close last-minute surveillance; it cannot be prepared ahead.

Grilled Yellow-Fin Tuna on Braised Greens with Beet Beurre Blanc

Serves 6
Prepare a charcoal fire or preheat the broiler

4 medium-size beets, peeled and
    cubed (about 2 cups)
2 cups water
Beurre Blanc, page 168
2 tablespoons heavy cream
Salt and freshly ground pepper
2 tablespoons butter
1 tablespoon finely chopped shallots
2 pounds beet greens or spinach,
    stemmed and torn into pieces
2 tablespoons dry white wine
6 yellow-fin tuna steaks,
    skinned and cut ¾ inch thick,
    about 6 ounces each
2 tablespoons olive oil

Combine the beets and water in a non-corrodible saucepan and simmer for 30 to 40 minutes, until the liquid is reduced to ½ cup. Strain the liquid into the shallot mixture in the Beurre Blanc and reduce by half; then proceed with the Beurre Blanc. Puree the beets with heavy cream and season with salt and pepper. Reserve and keep warm.

Heat the butter in a large skillet and cook the shallots for 1 minute, without browning. Add the greens and toss until they are coated with the butter and have begun to wilt. Sprinkle with the wine, cover the skillet tightly, and steam for 1 minute. Season with salt and pepper. Reserve and keep warm.

Brush the tuna with olive oil and season with salt and pepper. Grill or broil for 1½ to 2 minutes on each side, until medium-rare.

Ladle ¼ cup of beet beurre blanc onto each of 6 warmed serving plates. Drain the greens and divide them among the plates. Place the tuna on the bed of greens. Pipe beet puree in rosettes around the plates. Serve at once.

As served by Larry and Richard D'Amico, owners of Primavera, one of Minneapolis's most popular lunchtime restaurants, this dish has an almost neon look from the rich carmine of the beet-tinged sauce, accentuated by piped rosettes of contrasting vegetable purees, beet and hubbard squash, for instance, ranged around the plate. Look to the right—and be dazzled!

Baked Oysters with Cornbread-Tasso Dressing

Makes 24, serves 4–6
Preheat the oven to 400 degrees

3 cups chopped corn muffins or bread
2 tablespoons butter
⅓ cup finely chopped onion
⅓ cup finely chopped celery
⅓ cup finely chopped bell pepper
2 ounces finely chopped Tasso ham
(¼ cup plus 2 tablespoons)
1 jalapeño pepper, finely chopped
1½ cups Chicken Stock, page 166
½ cup heavy cream
½ teaspoon Worcestershire sauce
¼ teaspoon Tabasco sauce
24 oysters on the half shell, separated
¼ cup grated Parmesan cheese

Bentley's: one of those places where you are at home in black tie or your Sunday-morning sweater—or even your Saturday-afternoon one.

Place the corn muffins or bread on a pan and bake until they are lightly toasted, 5 to 10 minutes; it depends on the amount of moisture. Crumble the bread in a food processor.

Heat the butter in a skillet. Add the onion, celery and bell pepper and cook until softened, 3 to 5 minutes. Add ¼ cup of the Tasso ham and cook 2 minutes longer. Add the jalapeño and the breadcrumbs. Pour in the chicken stock and the cream. Cook, stirring frequently, until it is as thick as muffin batter, about 5 minutes. Season with the Worcestershire and the Tabasco and remove from the heat. If there are any juices with the oysters, pour them off into a wide skillet. Add water to the skillet to a depth of ½ inch. Bring the liquid to a simmer and poach the oysters, about 2 to 3 minutes. Do not crowd them in the pan. Drain them on paper towels.

Preheat the broiler.

Place an oyster in each shell. Top with about 1½ tablespoons of the cornbread-Tasso dressing, spreading it to cover the oyster. Sprinkle the oysters with the remaining Tasso and the Parmesan cheese. Broil the oysters until hot, bubbly and golden brown, 2 to 3 minutes. Serve at once.

NOTE: Tasso ham is spicy Cajun ham, cured with fennel, chili and other spices. It is available by mail order from Louisiana sources, and is sold in specialty food and gourmet shops.

As served at Bentley's in San Francisco, these oysters are addictive. No wonder the place always seems full of activity and good times.

95

Fresh Tuna Cooked on a Plate

Serves 2 as an appetizer

1 lemon
6 sprigs fresh thyme or ½ bunch
  Italian parsley
12 black oil-cured olives, such as
  Ligurian, Niçoise or Nyon
½ pound fresh tuna fillet, skinned
⅛ teaspoon salt
4 tablespoons extra-virgin
  olive oil

Cut the lemon in half and cut one half into very thin slices. Remove any seeds. Squeeze the other half and reserve the juice.

Reserve 2 of the thyme sprigs and remove the tiny leaves from the rest. Or, finely chop all but 2 sprigs of the parsley.

Pit the olives and chop them coarsely.

Using a very sharp knife, cut the tuna into 10 ¼-inch-thick slices, 3 inches long by ¾ inch wide. Toss the slices with the reserved lemon juice and the salt.

Cover the center of each of 2 flameproof plates with 1 tablespoon of the olive oil. Arrange 5 slices of tuna on each plate; beginning 2 inches from the edge of the plate, form a fan shape with the strips. Or, if the slices are shorter, arrange a sun burst from the center of the plate. Divide the lemon slices between the plates and sprinkle with the thyme or chopped parsley and the olives. Garnish with the thyme or parsley sprigs and drizzle each with a tablespoon of oil.

Place the plates directly on a gas burner, over a high flame, for about 30 seconds. The oil will sizzle slightly and the bottom of the tuna will just begin to cook while the top remains rare. Serve immediately.

This dish results directly from what has happened to the American marketplace. It is so simple that the ingredients must be superb for them to succeed. Before sushi became so popular, finding fresh tuna, filleted, was an unlikely event, while fresh thyme was mostly used by keen gardeners. The demand created by our increased interest in good food has made these once-obscure olives and extra-expensive extra-virgin oil both available—and appreciated. The chefs at Exile, a Manhattan bistro in TriBeCa, also serve fresh salmon prepared this way, substituting green picholine olives and capers for the black olives. Try presenting the fresh tuna on white flameproof plates and the salmon on black ones, as they do.

Sea Scallops with Watercress and Lime Beurre Blanc

Serves 4 as an appetizer

1 bunch watercress
1 quart water
1 cup dry white wine
1 small onion, sliced
½ stalk celery, sliced
3 slices lemon
3 parsley stems
¼ teaspoon dried thyme
1 whole clove
3 peppercorns
1 small bay leaf
Beurre Blanc, page 168
1 tablespoon fresh lime juice
16 large sea scallops
20 fresh raspberries

Remove the tough stems from the watercress and set aside 4 sprigs for garnish. Bring a saucepan of water to a boil and blanch the watercress for about 10 seconds, until the leaves are a brilliant green. Drain and cool under running water. Squeeze out the moisture and chop very finely. Reserve for the Beurre Blanc.

Combine the quart of water, wine, onion, celery, lemon, parsley stems, thyme, clove, peppercorns and bay leaf in a non-corrodible saucepan and bring to a boil. Reduce the heat and simmer for 20 minutes. Strain the mixture through a fine sieve and return it to the pan. Let it simmer very gently while you prepare the Beurre Blanc.

Prepare the Beurre Blanc and when all the butter has been incorporated, stir in the chopped watercress and the lime juice.

Poach the scallops in the simmering broth until they are firm and white, 2 to 3 minutes. Drain them and reserve the broth (court-bouillon) for another use.

Spoon ¼ cup of the sauce onto each of 4 warmed plates. Place 4 scallops in a circle on the sauce and surround with 5 of the raspberries. Place a sprig of watercress in the center of the plate and serve immediately.

Elegant and piquant, in a silken sauce that suits other seafood well, too, this is typical fare at Michael's, Santa Monica.

The Garden Restaurant now inhabits the handsome building in the heart of Philadelphia that once housed the Philadelphia Musical Academy. It does indeed have a garden and, at appropriate seasons, you can eat in it.

Bay Scallop Seviche

Serves 6

1½ teaspoons ground cumin
1 cup fresh lime juice
½ cup fresh orange juice
2 pounds bay scallops
1 hot red chili pepper, finely
    chopped
¼ cup finely chopped red onion
3 ripe plum tomatoes, seeded and
    chopped
1 sweet red pepper, seeded and
    chopped
3 scallions, chopped
1 cup chopped cilantro
1 lime, sliced, for garnish

Stir the cumin into the lime and orange juices and pour over the scallops. Stir in the chopped chili pepper and red onion. Cover and refrigerate for at least 2 hours.

    Just before serving, drain the scallops and mix with the chopped tomatoes, sweet pepper, scallions and cilantro. Garnish with the slices of lime.

Variations upon this classic dish are served just about everywhere these days. Seviches originated in countries where limes and fresh fish were plentiful and their appeal lies in the fact that the delicate flesh of the shellfish "cooks" in the acidic juice without toughening or ever losing its sweet succulence. They can be made in advance and assembled at the very last minute—and they also look beautiful. What perfect attributes!

The Garden's Red Snapper with Wild Mushrooms

Serves 4
Preheat the oven to 400 degrees

¾ pound shiitake mushrooms
8 tablespoons butter
3 tablespoons finely chopped shallots
1 tablespoon fresh lemon juice
Salt and freshly ground black pepper
4 unskinned red snapper fillets (about 6-7 ounces each)
1–2 teaspoons light olive oil
Beurre Blanc, page 168

Separate the shiitake stems and caps and slice the caps. Heat 4 tablespoons of the butter in a heavy skillet over moderate heat and sauté the mushrooms for about 5 minutes. Add 1 tablespoon of shallots and the lemon juice and sauté for 2 more minutes. Season to taste with salt and fresh black pepper. Keep warm.

Butter a cookie sheet with the remaining butter and sprinkle it with the remaining shallots. Arrange the snapper fillets in a crescent shape and bake in the upper part of the preheated oven for 12 minutes. Remove the fillets and brush with a few drops of olive oil to make them gleam.

Make a line of the mushrooms on each of 4 warmed plates. Cover with the snapper, skin side up, and serve in a pool of Beurre Blanc, with the mushrooms peeking from under the fish.

99

Grilled Halibut with Spiced Pepper Puree and Wild Mushrooms

Serves 2
Prepare a charcoal fire or preheat the broiler

2 yellow bell peppers, roasted and peeled
2 red bell peppers, roasted and peeled,
   see page 169 for method
1 tablespoon olive oil
1 shallot, finely chopped
2 garlic cloves, finely chopped
1 teaspoon fresh marjoram,
   or ½ teaspoon dried
1 teaspoon fresh oregano,
   or ½ teaspoon dried
1 tablespoon finely chopped fresh basil
Salt
½ teaspoon coarsely ground pepper
2 tablespoons butter
4 shiitake mushrooms, stems removed
4–8 chanterelles
   or other wild mushrooms
2 fillets of halibut,
   about 7 ounces each

Cut half a yellow and half a red pepper into thin strips and reserve them. Puree the rest of the yellow pepper, then the red, keeping the colored purees separate.

Heat 1 teaspoon of the oil in a small saucepan and add half the shallots and half the garlic. Cook until the shallots are soft and transparent, about 3 minutes. Add half of the marjoram, oregano and basil and the yellow pepper puree. Cook for 3 to 4 minutes, until the sauce thickens somewhat. Season to taste with salt and ¼ teaspoon of the ground pepper. Repeat the procedure to make a red pepper sauce.

Heat the butter in a heavy skillet and sauté the mushrooms until they are tender, about 6 minutes. Season with salt and pepper and keep warm.

Sprinkle the halibut lightly with salt and pepper and rub it with the remaining teaspoon of olive oil. Grill or broil it for about 4 minutes on each side, just until the fish starts to flake.

Place a spoonful of each of the pepper purees side by side on 2 plates. Center the fish on the purees. Garnish with the mushrooms and the reserved pepper strips.

Not the leanest diet food, but as made by Chef Walter Zuromski of Rarities in Boston, elegant and rewarding, with very few calories.

Shrimp Savannah

Serves 4–6

1 red bell pepper
1 green bell pepper
½ Spanish or Bermuda onion
8 tablespoons butter
1½ tablespoons finely chopped garlic
6 ounces firm country ham or
   prosciutto, cut into tiny dice (¾ cup)
2 teaspoons finely chopped
   fresh thyme
⅛ teaspoon cayenne pepper
2 pounds large shrimp, peeled and
   deveined, tails left intact
16 cherry tomatoes, halved
Salt and freshly ground pepper

Cut the peppers and onion into 1½-by-¼-inch strips and reserve.

Heat the butter in a 12-inch skillet over moderately high heat. Sprinkle in the garlic, then the ham, thyme and cayenne. Without stirring, spread the peppers and onion over this.

Place the shrimp, then the cherry tomatoes, on the vegetables. Cook for about 4 minutes, until the vegetables wilt and the shrimp begin to turn pink. Do not stir; just shake the pan gently.

Gently fold the shrimp into the vegetables, adding salt and pepper to taste. Continue shaking the pan for a minute or so, just until the shrimp are cooked through. Serve at once.

This recipe is from Elizabeth Terry, chef-owner of Elizabeth's on 37th Street in Savannah, Georgia, who serves it at her restaurant with a combination of white and wild rice, seasoned with a squeeze of lemon juice.

The Commander's Palace, said by many to be the best restaurant in New Orleans, has a special way with seafood. Below, a chef tends a vat of crawfish; at left, a shellfish setup in the sunny garden.

Caviar Pie

Serves 10–12

8 eggs
1–2 Spanish onions
3 cups sour cream
8–10 ounces caviar, such as
    golden American, salmon roe
    and any of the black caviars

Place the eggs in a heavy saucepan just large enough to hold them in a single layer. Cover them with water and place over moderate heat. Bring just to the boil; timing exactly from this moment, reduce the heat and keep the water at a bare simmer for 10 minutes. Rinse and cool the eggs in cold water, then shell them. You will need 5 whole eggs and 3 yolks. Reserve the 3 extra whites for another use. Chop the eggs finely.

Chop the onions to a medium-fine stage. You should have 2½ cups. Place a triple layer of paper towels on your work surface and cover it with the chopped onions. Roll it up tightly, jelly-roll fashion, squeezing as you roll. Press firmly to remove the liquid from the onions.

Spread the onions in an even layer in a 10-inch porcelain quiche dish. Then make an even layer of the chopped egg. Carefully spoon the sour cream over the eggs and smooth it with a spatula to bring it right to the edge and make it level.

Refrigerate for about 12 hours or overnight, until the "pie" has set. Top with the caviar just before serving. Cut into wedges to serve.

Chef Mark Militello, of Café Max in Pompano Beach, Florida, serves this in his restaurants—always. The bursting bubbles of caviar, buffered with a bed of the best sour cream you can find and layered with chopped eggs and Spanish onion, are self-contained in an open-faced "pie." Assemble the dish about 12 hours before you plan to serve it, and remember—it gets better with the quality of the caviar you top it with. Use black, red and golden, any or all.

Chefs travel far in pursuit of their calling and Caviar Pie was one of the delicacies Mark Militello made for a Matanzas Creek wine festival in California.

Salmon with Mustard, Horseradish and Dill

Serves 4 as an appetizer
Preheat the oven to 450 degrees

¾–1 pound fresh salmon fillet, skinned
¼ cup extra-virgin olive oil
   or melted butter
Salt and freshly ground white pepper
2 tablespoons dry white wine
8 teaspoons coarse-grained mustard,
   such as Moutarde de Meaux
4 teaspoons horseradish
½ cup fresh dill sprigs

Cut the salmon into very thin scallops on the diagonal.

Use the oil or butter to paint 4 *ovenproof* plates generously. Season the oil or butter with salt and pepper, and lay the salmon scallops on the plates, trimming them as needed so that the center of each plate is evenly covered, without any gaps.

Paint the salmon with the wine, or spray it, using a mister, then spread the fish with the mustard. Dot it liberally with the horseradish.

Strew the dill over the salmon and bake for 2 to 3 minutes, until it is just barely cooked; it will be opaque. The plates should be taken from the oven while the salmon is still underdone because it will continue to cook with the residual heat from the plates.

Serve at once.

Christopher Kump, a young chef at Café Beaujolais in Mendocino, California, developed this recipe for summer dinners, to take advantage of the local bounty of the handsome Pacific king salmon, with its dazzling vermilion-colored flesh. He prepares it on large flat appetizer plates, 9½ inches in diameter, with a 6½-inch center, and a rim decorated with morning glories. These plates can be prepared some hours ahead and then cooked at the last moment.

Down Home Cooking

Did you ever say to yourself, "I'm so hungry?" And you wanted to be fed something simple and good, and right away? Then rejoice, because down home cooking is back in style, and when we need babying a whole crowd of chefs are eager to take up where Mom left off.

Comfort foods taste good in all kinds of settings: a totally straightforward sandwich-salad-pie setup at a New York diner; the gratification of eating—if not actually IN bed, at least on a table made out of one, at Skobey's in Kingsport, Tennessee; or the sweet simplicity of a table for two at The Inn at Pawleys Island, South Carolina, where the enticing scents from the kitchen are backed by the smell of the sea.

Whose home are we talking about here? Our own, of course, where each one of us was imprinted with the foods that made—and still make—us comfortable. Down home is not just a concept of mashed potatoes; maybe mashed potatoes was not what made *you* feel good. Maybe it was kielbasa and cabbage, or collard greens and pot likker. But in the American Bistro, purveyors of just about all the foods you loved when you were a kid are out there looking for you.

They say that you *can* go home again, back to your roots, and sure enough, you can get creamed chicken and biscuits, or pork roasted as your Tuscan grandmother used to do it. Pot pies are back in, and custards too (though sometimes gentrified as crème brûlée).

They are also recreating the popular haunts of yesterday—notably the diner, with its appealing proposition that you can eat anything you want at any time of the night or day. And why not? Bacon and eggs and pecan pie at three in the morning? Who says you can't? A big thick white china cup of coffee with a rim you can hardly get your mouth around? And do let's have some good, old-fashioned creamy rice pudding.

Now we are eating more and more meals out, restaurants are the places where we gather—in the eclecticism of the American Bistro, we can feel at home, too, and there will always be one where the mood exactly matches our own and the food is just what we fancy.

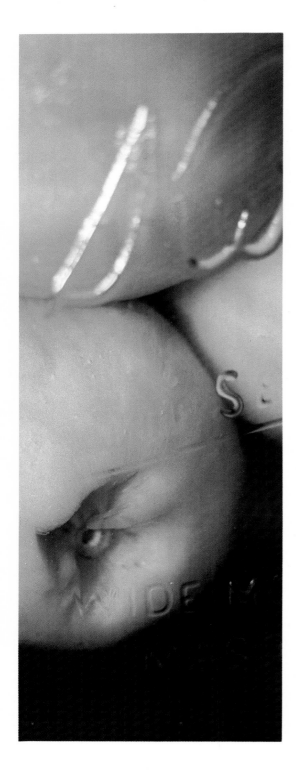

Oyster Loaf

Makes 12–24 slices

2 cups shucked fresh oysters
1-pound loaf long French bread
¼ cup olive oil
1 ripe tomato, seeded and chopped
4 scallions, chopped
¼ cup chopped black olives
¼ cup chopped stuffed green olives
1½ tablespoons finely chopped garlic
2 tablespoons finely chopped parsley
2 tablespoons drained and chopped capers
2 tablespoons fresh lemon juice
1 teaspoon chopped fresh thyme, or ⅛ teaspoon dried
¼ teaspoon Tabasco sauce
½ cup grated Parmesan cheese

Garnish:

6–8 green leaves such as kale, romaine or escarole
6–8 parsley sprigs
12 black olives

Poach the oysters in their own liquor (add water if there is insufficient oyster liquor) until they just curl up around the edges, about 3 minutes. Drain the oysters and spread on paper towels to cool. When they have cooled, chop them coarsely.

Cut the bread in half lengthwise, and hollow it out, leaving 2 shells about ¼ inch thick. Grind the crumbs coarsely and paint the insides of the shells with 2 to 3 tablespoons of the olive oil; make sure to paint right up to the edges.

Combine the breadcrumbs, the chopped oysters and all the remaining ingredients and mix them together, lightly but thoroughly.

Pack the stuffing firmly into the bread shells, keeping it flush with the edges and mounded slightly in the center. Press the halves together and place the loaf on a very large piece of aluminum foil, big enough to encircle the loaf twice. Roll the loaf snugly in the foil and twist the ends shut. Secure the foil by wrapping masking tape firmly around the loaf in 2 or 3 places. Refrigerate the stuffed loaf overnight, or up to 24 hours.

To serve, unwrap the loaf and cut it into crosswise slices ¼ to ½ inch thick. Line a large flat basket or tray with the green leaves and arrange the slices in overlapping concentric circles. Garnish with parsley and black olives.

At The Ark, a seaside restaurant in Nahcotta, Washington, co-owner Jimella Lucas offers this delicious interpretation of a recipe with a long and honorable history. In the days when oysters were plentiful, it was a cheap, easy and delicious dish. Though the first adjective no longer applies, the others still do. Try it and see.

Down home can be as simple as spiced peaches in a Ball jar, or as friendly as lunchtime at the bar at the Dixie Café in San Francisco.

Creamed Chicken and Biscuits

Serves 2

Biscuits, page 114
½ pound boneless, skinless
   chicken breast
3 button mushrooms
3 shiitake or other wild mushrooms
1 tablespoon butter
1 tablespoon finely chopped
   red bell pepper
1 tablespoon finely chopped
   green bell pepper
½ tablespoon finely chopped
   jalapeño pepper
¾ cup heavy cream
Salt and freshly ground pepper

Have the biscuits ready to slip into the oven to bake as you begin to prepare the chicken.

Cut the chicken into ½-inch-wide strips. Slice the mushrooms, and if you are using shiitakes, discard the stems. Heat the butter in a skillet; when it stops foaming, add the chicken and mushrooms and sauté over moderate heat for 4 minutes. Add the peppers and cook, stirring, over high heat for 1 more minute.

Pour the cream into the skillet and cook until it has reduced and thickened, about 5 minutes. Season with salt and pepper.

To serve, split 4 warm biscuits and divide them between 2 plates. Cover them with the creamed chicken.

Chef Billy Della Ventura of the 95th Restaurant in Chicago adds the sophisticated touch of using wild mushrooms to this lovely homey fare—and it is splendidly simple to make.

Louisiana French Toast

Makes 8 pieces

1 orange
1 cup milk
½ cup heavy cream
⅓ cup fresh orange juice
2 tablespoons sugar
2 eggs, beaten
½ teaspoon cinnamon
½ teaspoon vanilla extract
1 large loaf French bread
8 tablespoons butter
¼ cup confectioners' sugar

Trim the ends of the orange and cut it into thin slices. Cut each slice in half and set aside.

Combine the milk, cream, orange juice, sugar, eggs, cinnamon, and vanilla in a large bowl and mix well. Cut the bread, on the extreme diagonal, into 8 thick slices. Dip each slice in turn into the bowl, making sure it is well soaked, then squeeze it gently to get rid of the excess liquid.

Heat the butter in a large heavy skillet and when it is foaming, add the soaked bread. Cook over moderate heat for about 5 minutes, then turn and cook for 3 minutes on the second side, or until golden. Drain on paper towels.

Sprinkle the toast with confectioners' sugar and arrange on plates, garnished with the orange slices.

One need no longer travel to New England or New Orleans to taste their regional specialties. Like the recipe opposite, this dish can be tasted in the heart of Manhattan—in this case, at the American Festival Café in Rockefeller Center, which takes pride in the variety of its fresh, seasonal American food.

Martha's Vineyard Corn Pudding

Serves 6
Preheat the oven to 350 degrees

3 tablespoons butter
6 ears fresh sweet corn, husked
2 eggs, lightly beaten
½ cup milk
¾ teaspoon salt
¼ teaspoon freshly ground pepper

Melt 2 tablespoons of the butter and use half of it to coat six 6-ounce custard cups or ramekins; place them in a baking pan in which they will fit without touching.

Slit each row of corn kernels lengthwise down the center. Use the blunt edge of a knife to scrape the kernels downward into a large bowl.

Stir the eggs, milk, salt, pepper and the remaining melted butter into the corn and ladle the mixture into the buttered cups. Fill the baking pan with 1 inch of tap water and bake the custards for 25 to 30 minutes, until set. A knife tip inserted in the center of a cup should come out clean.

Slice the remaining tablespoon of butter into 6 thin pats and place 1 on each pudding. Serve at once, with the butter just beginning to melt.

These delicate little ramekins capture the fresh pure taste of sweet corn with melted butter and nothing more. Chef Walter Plendner, who created them for the American Harvest Restaurant in New York City, where foods are served only at the height of their season, warns that when it is sweet corn time, the kernels will be so full of milk that you will need only a few drops of the dairy variety.

All foods are enhanced by the right decor, and down home cooking offers countless opportunities to an inventive restaurateur— whether it is serving grilled sausages on a platter from the 1930s or chilling guests' wine in a tin pail.

Catfish Beignets

Serves 4

Sauce:

½ cup mayonnaise, preferably homemade
2 tablespoons sour cream
1½ teaspoons Dijon mustard
Salt and freshly ground pepper

1¼ pounds catfish fillets,
    cut into ½-inch cubes
6 tablespoons Louisiana-style
    hot sauce or 3 tablespoons Tabasco
Vegetable oil for deep-frying
¾ cup flour
¼ cup cornstarch
1 teaspoon sweet paprika
½ teaspoon cayenne pepper
2 teaspoons salt
⅛ teaspoon garlic powder
4 Boston or bibb lettuce leaves
1½ tablespoons finely chopped parsley

Combine the sauce ingredients as long as a day ahead of serving, to give the flavors a chance to develop. Cover and refrigerate.

Marinate the catfish in the pepper sauce for 1 to 4 hours, refrigerated. The longer the fish marinates, the spicier it gets.

Fill a deep-fryer or a saucepan with oil to a depth of 4 inches. Heat the oil to 350 degrees.

Combine the flour, cornstarch, paprika, cayenne, salt and garlic powder in a large shallow bowl. When the oil is ready, dip the fish in the seasoned flour, shake off any excess, and fry a handful at a time, for about 2 minutes, until the pieces rise to the top of the oil. Skim out the fish and drain it on paper towels.

Place a lettuce leaf on each of 4 plates and fill each leaf with a few spoonfuls of sauce. Sprinkle the sauce with parsley. Divide the beignets among the plates and serve at once.

At Mr. B's in New Orleans, a sprightly restaurant owned by the Brennans, the royal family of New Orleans cuisine, these golden puffs are made either with redfish or catfish. Redfish stocks are dwindling as their reputation becomes more and more blackened, so I suggest using catfish, now being aquacultured in Mississippi and sold in vast quantities nationwide.

Shad Roe with Country Ham

Serves 2 as an entree;
serves 4 as an appetizer
Preheat the oven to 400 degrees

8 slices of country ham or
Smithfield ham, thinly cut,
about 6 ounces total
6 tablespoons butter, melted
2 pairs of shad roe
¼ cup flour
Freshly ground black pepper
1 lemon, cut into wedges

The sandwich: not just the cornerstone of down home cooking, but the bricks and mortar too. Could this have been what Shakespeare meant when he wrote, "O wall, Show me thy chink?"

Bring a large pot of water to a boil, reduce the heat and add the ham. Simmer for 3 minutes, to remove some of the saltiness. Drain and dry the ham.

Brush a baking dish with 3 tablespoons of the butter. Dredge the roes in the flour, sprinkle with pepper and place them in the buttered dish. Cover and bake for 7 minutes.

Uncover the roes, brush them with butter and cover with the ham. Brush the ham with butter and return the dish to the oven. Bake, uncovered, for 5 minutes; baste with butter and bake for a final 5 minutes. Serve, garnished with lemon wedges.

When the shad begin their spring run, the American Festival Cafe starts serving this recipe in their Sea Grill—and guests have been known to come to Rockefeller Center just to taste it.

Stuffed Monterey Jack

Serves 6
Preheat the oven to 350 degrees

2 tablespoons olive oil
1 cup chopped onions
1 clove garlic, finely chopped
1¼ pounds lean ground beef
½ cup dry white wine
1 cup chicken broth
1 teaspoon salt
⅛ teaspoon red pepper flakes
1 teaspoon ground cumin
½ cup chopped red bell pepper
½ cup chopped green bell pepper
½ cup seedless raisins
½ cup sliced almonds
1 cup cooked rice
1 tablespoon cornstarch
2 tablespoons water
1 pound thinly sliced
   Monterey Jack cheese
2 tablespoons breadcrumbs

Use a little of the oil to coat a 3-quart soufflé dish.

Heat the remaining oil in a large heavy skillet. Add the onion and garlic and cook until the onion is translucent. Add the beef and brown it quickly. Pour out any fat that has accumulated and pour in the wine; cook for 1 minute on high heat, stirring. Add the broth, salt, pepper flakes and cumin and mix well. Reduce the heat, cover the pan and simmer for 30 minutes.

Add the peppers, raisins, almonds and rice to the skillet and stir until most of the liquid is absorbed. Combine the cornstarch and water and quickly stir it into the mixture. Remove the pan from the heat and let it cool almost to room temperature, stirring occasionally.

Line the oiled soufflé dish with the cheese, overlapping the slices by ¼ inch. Spoon the cooled mixture into the dish and press down lightly. Chop any remaining cheese and distribute it over the surface, then sprinkle with the breadcrumbs.

Place the dish in a hot-water bath and bake for 45 minutes. Remove from the oven and set the soufflé dish aside to rest for 20 minutes. Unmold the dish, gently and carefully, onto a warm serving platter.

I asked Tom Margittai, co-owner of The Four Seasons, for one of Chef Seppi Renggli's recipes for this section, and he suggested this—a tasty cross between a good meatloaf and moussaka—to be served with boiled potatoes.

Pork Roast (Arista)

Serves 6–8
Preheat the oven to 350 degrees

6 cloves garlic, finely chopped
1–2 tablespoons fennel seeds
2 teaspoons coarse salt
Freshly ground pepper
4 pound boneless pork loin roast
Fruity olive oil

Make a paste with the garlic, fennel, salt and pepper. If the roast is tied, unroll it. Spread most of the paste over the inside of the meat, reserving 1 tablespoon. Roll and tie the roast so that the pale tenderloin is centered, surrounded by the darker meat of the loin. Make a few incisions in the roast and stuff some of the paste into them. Rub any remaining paste over the meat, then paint it with olive oil.

Place the meat in a roasting pan and roast, uncovered, for about 2 hours, or until the internal temperature registers 170 degrees. Baste the roast several times.

Remove the meat from the oven and let it cool at room temperature. When it is tepid, cut it into ½-inch-thick slices and serve, sprinkled with a few drops of olive oil.

NOTE: *Arista* is the Tuscan name for this dish.

Evan Kleiman (left), the chef/co-owner of Angeli Caffe/Pizzeria in Los Angeles, likes to serve this succulent roast at room temperature (opposite). In every way it conjures up a sense of the Italian countryside, say, at the time of the vintage, when the new wine flows from the village fountain and the winding streets are filled with stalls selling slices of just such richly aromatic meats as this.

Cheese Biscuits

Makes 18–20
Preheat the oven to 425 degrees

2 cups flour
⅓ cup non-fat dry milk powder
2½ tablespoons wheat germ
1 tablespoon baking powder
¾ teaspoon salt
3 tablespoons grated white
  cheddar cheese (preferably raw milk)
2 tablespoons grated mozzarella cheese
2 tablespoons grated Emmenthal
  or Swiss cheese
8 tablespoons chilled butter, cut
  into pieces
1 cup cold water

Combine all the dry ingredients in the container of a food processor. Pulse to mix well. Add the 3 cheeses and turn machine on and off just to mix. Add the butter and pulse a few times to cut it into small pieces. With the machine running, add the water all at once. The moment it is incorporated, turn off the machine.

Lightly flour a work surface and pat the dough into an 8-by-16-inch rectangle. Use a floured knife to cut it into 2½-inch squares. Arrange the biscuits evenly on a non-stick baking sheet and bake for about 15 minutes, until lightly colored. Serve warm.

At Elizabeth's on 37th Street in Savannah, Georgia, owner Elizabeth Terry offers savory, wheat-flecked biscuits that are quite out of the ordinary.

Biscuits

Makes 10–12
Preheat the oven to 400 degrees

2 cups flour
2½ teaspoons baking powder
½ teaspoon salt
6 tablespoons butter, at room temperature
1 cup milk
1 egg, lightly beaten

Lightly butter a baking sheet.

Sift the flour, baking powder and salt together into a bowl. Add the butter and break it up into small pieces with a fork. Add ¾ cup of the milk and mix well.

Flour a board and rolling pin, and roll out the dough about ¾-inch thick. Use a cookie cutter or drinking glass to cut the dough into 2- to 3-inch circles and arrange them, 2 inches apart, on the prepared sheet.

Combine the egg with the remaining milk and brush onto the dough. Bake for 15 to 17 minutes, until the biscuits are golden. Serve warm.

A classic accompaniment to the Creamed Chicken on page 107, and wonderful, buttered, with strawberry preserves or country ham.

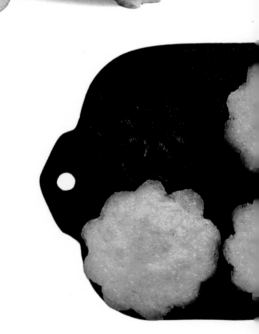

Cottage Cheese Dill Rolls

Makes 18 rolls

¼-ounce package active dry yeast
¼ cup warm water
2 tablespoons sugar
1 cup cottage cheese,
    at room temperature
1 tablespoon finely chopped onion
2 teaspoons dried dill weed
1 teaspoon salt
1 egg
2½ cups flour

Dissolve the yeast in warm water and stir in the sugar. Stir in the remaining ingredients and mix to form a dough. Knead the dough until it is firm and elastic and place it in a buttered bowl. Cover the bowl and let the dough rise in a warm place for 2 hours, or until doubled in size.

Lightly butter a baking sheet.

Punch down the dough and shape it into 18 round pieces. Place them on the cookie sheet, cover and let rise for 1 hour. Preheat the oven to 400 degrees.

Bake the rolls for 10 to 15 minutes, until golden, and serve warm.

A version of classical Americana as presented by Chef James Heywood at the American Bounty Restaurant in Hyde Park, New York. The restaurant is run by the Culinary Institute of America and serves as a training ground for its students, many of whom have already made culinary history.

Muffins are as American as pie, and these days they turn up on bistro tables everywhere. At Sarabeth's newest Kitchen (right) on Manhattan's West Side, diners *must* run a gauntlet of baked goods so fresh that the steam still mists the display case—and not many get by without stopping to buy some.

Honey-Bran Muffins

Makes 12 muffins
Preheat the oven to 400 degrees

1½ cups flour
1½ cups bran
1 tablespoon baking soda
½ teaspoon salt
¼ teaspoon freshly ground nutmeg
2 eggs
1 cup buttermilk
¼ cup honey
1 cup packed brown sugar
6 tablespoons melted butter
½ cup chopped dates

Butter a 12-cup muffin tin or line it with paper muffin cups.

Combine the flour, bran, soda, salt and nutmeg in a large bowl and mix well. In a separate bowl, whisk together the eggs, buttermilk, honey, brown sugar and butter until smooth. Toss the dates with a tablespoonful of the dry ingredients.

Make a well in the center of the dry ingredients and pour in the liquid ingredients all at once. Combine the mixtures just until the dry ingredients are moistened. Fold the dates gently into the batter and allow it to rest for 2 to 3 minutes.

Spoon the batter into the prepared muffin tin; the cups should be about three-quarters full. Bake the muffins for about 15 to 20 minutes, or until golden brown. If they are browning too quickly, reduce the heat to 375 degrees. When they are done, a toothpick inserted in the center will come out clean. Serve warm.

At The Ark, in Nahcotta, Washington, co-owners Jimella Lucas and Nanci Main serve up a boatful of simple, gorgeous foods in a sea-girt setting. Nanci's moist, light muffins demand a 400-degree setting or they'll sink.

118

Herbed Dumplings

Makes 12–18

1 cup flour
2 teaspoons baking powder
½ teaspoon salt
½ cup milk
2 tablespoons vegetable oil
1 tablespoon finely chopped parsley
1 tablespoon finely chopped chives,
    tarragon or thyme

Combine the flour, baking powder and salt in a bowl. Mix the milk, oil and herbs together and add them to the bowl. Stir the mixture just enough to moisten the dry ingredients evenly.

Drop the batter by tablespoons, about ½ inch apart, into simmering liquid; this can be the Rabbit Stew, page 73, a soup or broth, another stew, or simply salted water. Cover the pan tightly and cook, undisturbed, for 10 to 15 minutes, until the dumplings are firm and dry in the center.

If they have been cooked in water, drain and serve them with melted butter. If they have been cooked in a stew or soup, they will be an integral part of that dish.

One tends to forget how useful dumplings can be: a pleasantly light, fluffy complement to a strongly flavored stew or soup, with the biscuit's advantage of cooking quickly, and the added bonus of lurking ready to serve under the same lid as the main dish. These come from the country bistro, Freshfields, in West Cornwall, Connecticut.

Hush Puppies

Makes 24–30
Preheat the oven to 200 degrees

2 cups cornmeal
1 cup flour
1 teaspoon baking soda
1 tablespoon baking powder
1 teaspoon salt
6 tablespoons very finely
    chopped onion
2 eggs
2 cups buttermilk
¼ teaspoon hot pepper sauce
Vegetable oil for frying

Mix the cornmeal, flour, baking soda, baking powder and salt in a bowl. Combine the onion, eggs, buttermilk and the pepper sauce in another bowl and beat with a fork until well mixed. Pour the liquid into the dry ingredients and combine to make a smooth batter. Do not overmix. Cover the bowl and let the batter rest for 20 minutes.

Heat 2 to 3 inches of oil in a skillet until it is very hot, but not smoking, about 375 degrees. Line a large pan with several thicknesses of paper towels and place it in the preheated oven.

To make the hush puppies, scoop up a rounded teaspoon of the batter and push it into the hot oil with another spoon. Fry the fritters 4 to 6 at a time, flipping them over once, until they are golden and float high on the surface of the oil, about 1½ minutes on each side. Transfer each batch to the towel-lined pan and serve as soon as they are all cooked.

When we cook down home, hush puppies take an honored place at table and these melting mouthfuls can strut their stuff in the highest society.

Pages 116-7: Friend-ships bloom along with the flowers in the informal atmosphere of Chez Panisse.

Bread Pudding Soufflé with Whiskey Sauce

Serves 6
Preheat the oven to 350 degrees

Bread Pudding:

9 1-inch-thick slices French bread,
   crusts removed
1¼ cups heavy cream
⅓ cup sugar
5 tablespoons butter, melted
   and cooled
⅛ teaspoon freshly grated nutmeg
⅛ teaspoon cinnamon
2 teaspoons vanilla extract
2 tablespoons raisins

Soufflé:

6 egg yolks, beaten
¼ cup sugar
6 egg whites
½ cup confectioners' sugar

Whiskey Sauce:

2 tablespoons sugar
1½ cups heavy cream
⅛ teaspoon vanilla extract
1½ teaspoons cornstarch
2 tablespoons water
4 teaspoons bourbon
1 tablespoon butter, cut into pieces

Arrange the bread slices in a 9-by-9-by-1¾-inch baking pan. Combine the remaining pudding ingredients and pour over the bread. Let it sit for 5 minutes and turn the bread slices. Let it sit for 10 more minutes, so that the pudding mixture soaks into the bread.

Cover the pan with aluminum foil and place it in a larger pan. Fill this pan with hot water, up to ½ inch from the top of the bread-pudding pan. Bake for 35 minutes, then remove the foil and bake for 10 to 15 minutes longer, to lightly brown the top. The custard should still be somewhat soft. Let it cool to room temperature.

Prepare the soufflé mixture. Put the egg yolks and sugar in the top of a double boiler set over, not in, simmering water. Whisk until the mixture is thick and lemon-colored. Combine the yolk mixture with the cooled bread pudding in a large bowl.

Turn up the oven heat to 375 degrees.

Beat the egg whites until very frothy. Gradually add the confectioners' sugar, beating constantly, until the mixture stands in almost stiff, but still moist, peaks. Add about ½ cup of the beaten egg whites to the bread pudding-egg yolk mixture, to lighten it, then gently fold the remaining egg whites into the bread pudding mixture, without deflating the whites.

Butter and lightly sugar a 2½-quart soufflé dish. Fill it with the bread pudding mixture. Bake it for 25 to 30 minutes, or until the top is golden brown and the soufflé is slightly moist.

About 5 minutes before the soufflé is ready, make the Whiskey Sauce. Slowly heat the sugar, cream and vanilla in a heavy saucepan, stirring often, until the mixture just starts to boil. Remove the pan from the heat. Dissolve the cornstarch in the water and stir this into the cream until it is thickened. Add the bourbon and slowly beat in the butter to finish the sauce.

Serve with the warm soufflé.

Bread puddings have reappeared in new forms, lightened and enriched by such master chefs as Emeril Lagasse of The Commander's Palace in New Orleans, a place where (right) they know how to let the good times roll.

Versatile darling of the new American cooking is the raspberry, most fragile and luxurious of fruits, with an inimitable sweet-tart fragrance and cushiony softness (marred for some only by its tiny tooth-hugging seeds).

Raspberry and Apple Bread Pudding

Serves 8
Preheat the oven to 350 degrees

4 eggs
¾ cup sugar
⅓ cup flour
3 cups heavy cream
4 brioches (about ½ pound)
2 medium-size green apples
1 tablespoon butter
1 pint raspberries (or sliced
  strawberries)
2 tablespoons sifted
  confectioners' sugar

Stir together the eggs, sugar and flour and add the cream gradually to form a smooth mixture.

Trim the crusts from the brioches. Cut them into slices and then into triangles. Peel, core and slice the apples.

Butter a 1½-quart soufflé dish and layer a third of the brioche slices in it. Cover with a layer of half the apple slices. Add a third of the egg custard. Arrange another layer of a third of the brioche, the remaining apples and all of the berries. Slowly add the remaining custard and cover with the remaining brioche slices and the rest of the custard.

Bake for 50 to 60 minutes, until the custard has set and the brioche is delicately browned.

Sprinkle with the confectioners' sugar and serve at room temperature.

A surprising, delicate and delicious combination of flavors. Rarely has bread pudding tasted so good as in this recipe from Chef Jim Dodge of Fournou's Ovens at the Stanford Court Hotel in San Francisco.

Strawberry Shortcake

Serves 6
Preheat the oven to 400 degrees

Shortcakes:

2 cups flour, lightly spooned
   and measured
1 tablespoon baking powder
¼ teaspoon salt
½ cup vegetable shortening
½ cup cold heavy cream

Strawberries:

1½ quarts ripe strawberries
About 6 tablespoons superfine sugar

½ cup heavy cream
1½ tablespoons butter

Combine the flour, baking powder and salt in a large mixing bowl. Cut in the shortening until the mixture resembles coarse meal. Drizzle ¼ cup of the cream over the top and quickly stir it in with a fork, just until blended. Add the remaining ¼ cup cream and stir to make a soft dough. If the dough is too dry, sprinkle it with a few drops of cold water.

Pat out the dough on a lightly floured surface to a thickness of about 1 inch. Using a 2½-inch biscuit cutter, cut out 5 shortcakes. Gather the scraps of dough and pat them together; cut out the sixth cake. Place the shortcakes on an ungreased baking sheet and bake for 15 to 18 minutes, until they are light golden brown. (Make sure not to open the oven door during the first 12 minutes of cooking.) Cool them slightly, but serve while they are still warm.

Choose the 6 prettiest berries for garnish, and rinse and hull all the berries, halving or quartering the large ones. Place them in a large bowl and crush gently. Add the sugar, stirring to dissolve, then taste and add more sugar, if needed. Place a sieve over a bowl and drain the crushed berries, pressing gently to extract some of the juice.

Whip the ½ cup of cream until it is stiff.

Split the warm shortcakes, placing the bottom halves in shallow soup bowls. Cut the butter into 6 thin slices and place a slice on each cake. Cover with the tops and let the butter melt for a minute. Remove the tops, spoon the drained crushed berries over the shortcakes, then replace the tops. Spoon the juice over each shortcake in turn and garnish with whipped cream and a whole strawberry.

A great recipe for a simple American classic, as served by Walter Plendner, executive chef at the American Harvest in Manhattan's Vista Hotel.

In city and country, bistro tables set out to delight as many senses as possible: at right, a quiet corner at The Ballroom in New York where the sculpture takes off from Matisse; at left, the garden at Dudley's in Lexington, Kentucky, provides the utmost in sweet pleasures—and a fountain too.

Creamed Rice Pudding

Serves 8–12

1 quart half-and-half
2 cups heavy cream
⅔ cup long grain white rice
⅔ cup sugar
⅛ teaspoon salt
1 vanilla bean, split, or
  2 teaspoons vanilla extract
3 egg yolks
⅓ cup raisins
3 tablespoons dark rum
1 teaspoon ground cinnamon

Combine the half-and-half and 1½ cups of the heavy cream in a large heavy saucepan. Stir in the rice, sugar, salt and vanilla bean, if you are using it. Place the pan over moderate heat and, stirring constantly, bring the mixture to a boil. Do not let it boil over. Reduce the heat to low and simmer, stirring frequently, until it is as thick as oatmeal, about 35 minutes. Stir constantly during the last 10 minutes to prevent sticking. Remove the pan from the heat.

Whisk the egg yolks in a large bowl and gradually add about 1 cup of the pudding; then add the rest. Stir in the vanilla extract if you are using it. Cover with plastic wrap, placed directly on the surface, then cool, and chill thoroughly, preferably overnight.

Combine the raisins and rum in a small bowl and let them soak for at least an hour, preferably overnight.

Whip the remaining ½ cup of heavy cream until stiff and carefully fold it into the chilled rice pudding.

Drain the raisins and spoon a few into individual serving bowls. Sprinkle with cinnamon and spoon ½ to ¾ cup of the pudding into each dish, over the raisins. Serve cold.

A gloriously creamy recipe from Bruce Auden at Charley's 517 in Houston.

Blackberry Grunt

Serves 6
Preheat the oven to 375 degrees

3 cups blackberries or
    other berries, or sliced fruit
⅓ cup sugar
¼ teaspoon cinnamon
¼ teaspoon nutmeg
¼ teaspoon ground cloves
¼ cup molasses
2 tablespoons lemon juice

Topping:
1 cup flour
1½ teaspoons baking powder
3 tablespoons cold butter
1 tablespoon vegetable oil
1 egg, lightly beaten
¼ cup milk
1 egg yolk for the glaze

Wash the berries carefully and combine them with the sugar, spices, molasses and lemon juice. Transfer to a deep, 9-inch baking dish.

Prepare the biscuit topping: Sift the flour with the baking powder and salt. Cut in the butter and oil with a pastry blender or with your fingertips until the mixture resembles coarse crumbs. Stir together the egg and 1 tablespoon of the milk and add to the flour mixture. Add another drop or two of milk if necessary to form a soft dough.

Roll the dough out lightly on a floured surface to about ½ inch thick and stamp out circles of dough, using a biscuit cutter. Cover the berries with the dough circles. Make a glaze by combining the egg yolk with the remaining milk and brush this mixture over the surface of the dough.

Bake, uncovered, in the preheated oven for 25 minutes until nicely browned.

Serve alone hot, or at room temperature or with a small scoop of crème fraîche, whipped cream or ice cream.

This recipe comes from Richard Perry's Restaurant in St. Louis, and I adore it. The flavors of the fruit are amazingly intensified by the spices and the biscuit crust makes an ideal contrast to the darkly aromatic, juicy filling.

Baked Stuffed Apples

Serves 6
Preheat the oven to 325 degrees

6 small apples
¼ cup golden raisins
¼ cup dark raisins
½ cup dark rum
¼ cup chopped walnuts
⅓ cup honey
2 tablespoons butter
¼ cup confectioners' sugar
1 cup heavy cream

Butter a baking dish that the apples will fit into snugly. Soak the raisins in ⅓ cup of the rum for 30 minutes. Peel a wide band of skin from the top of each apple and use a melon baller to scoop out the core without piercing the bottom. Arrange the apples in the dish.

Stir the nuts and honey into the raisin-rum mixture and divide the mixture among the apples, pressing it down well into each cavity. Top each apple with a teaspoon of butter. Bake in the lower part of the preheated oven for 30 minutes, basting frequently with the pan juices. Allow to cool for 30 minutes before serving.

Add the confectioners' sugar and the remaining rum to the cream and whip into soft peaks. Serve with the apples.

One of the oldest of recipes, and one of the best, updated to suit the contemporary taste for slightly less sweet, infinitely comforting desserts.

In the flower-filled hall of their Inn at Little Washington, deep in the Virginia country-side, co-owners Reinhard Lynch and Chef Patrick O'Connell adopt traditional poses—and so does a friend in the foreground.

Anything Goes (in the Kitchen)!

hen chefs really get going the surprises start coming. How about trying great-grandmother's recipe for wild greens, or a cheesecake made from goat cheese, hazelnuts and raspberries, or lamb sausage with watercress, or tortilla soup. Really? Yes, really.

Bistro chefs enjoy being explorers as well as artists in the kitchen, contrasting the whimsical with dazzling technique to pull off surprise after surprise. It is as if they can only justify taking the time to sleep by dreaming up another dish to delight and amuse us.

In fact, very few of the dishes that we were accustomed to seeing five years ago now survive on their menus, and most of those have been transmuted through some lively imaginations. American chefs are constantly recombining elements, presenting new and old ingredients in new ways, applying traditional and nontraditional cooking methods to serve forth foods with fresh touches.

The hard work of running a restaurant never changes—the problems are the same, the hours are as long. Yet something about the attitude, it seems, *has* changed. It is all a wonderfully exhilarating lark and every night it is different.

The quality that makes good restaurants great is that of caring. Chefs are not carefully trained artisans, producing formula food night after night. Every dinner will have its surprises for the evening's specials, and menus that reflect the changing seasons. The relentless search for new ingredients never ends—especially those that are locally produced and brought daily to the restaurant door by the growers, the fish smokers and the bakers themselves.

The flavors are pure and intense, the colors are vivid, and the presentations sublime—yet their patterns change like kaleidoscopes at the stroke of each midnight clock.

Who knows what's next?

Anything goes.

In Williamsburg, at The Trellis, beautiful ingredients dress the windows; at Pawleys Island Inn, owner Louis Osteen, a former actor, now performs at the stove; at John Byron's in Milwaukee, Chef Sandy D'Amato poses *beneath* his beautiful food.

Tortilla Soup

Makes about 2 quarts; serves 6–8

2 medium-size onions
(about ½ pound)
3 ripe, medium-size tomatoes
(about 1 pound)
1 tablespoon corn oil
2 corn tortillas, chopped
4 cloves garlic, finely chopped
½ branch epazote, optional
1 tablespoon ground cumin
1 teaspoon chili powder
1 bay leaf
2 tablespoons tomato puree
2 quarts Chicken Stock, page 166
Salt
⅛ teaspoon cayenne pepper

Garnishes:

4 corn tortillas
3 tablespoons corn oil
Salt
½ pound skinless, boneless
chicken breasts, poached
and cut into ¼-inch strips
1 cup coarsely grated cheddar cheese
1 firm, but ripe avocado, peeled
and cut into ½-inch cubes

Peel and quarter the onions and core and quarter the tomatoes. Puree them in a food processor or blender and reserve.

Heat the 1 tablespoon of corn oil in a large saucepan. When it is hot, add the chopped corn tortillas, garlic and the optional epazote. Sauté for 3 minutes. Add the pureed onions and tomatoes and stir over moderate heat until the mixture boils. Add the cumin, chili powder, bay leaf, tomato puree and stock. Bring to a boil and add salt to taste and the cayenne pepper. Reduce the heat and simmer for 30 minutes, stirring occasionally.

Place a sieve over a large bowl and pour the soup through it. Stir the mixture in the sieve, but do not force it through. Discard any pulp remaining in the strainer. Return the soup to the pot and keep hot.

To prepare the tortillas for garnishing, cut them in half, stack the halves and cut them across into ½-inch strips. Heat the 3 tablespoons of corn oil in a heavy skillet. Fry the strips, a few at a time, until crisp and golden brown on both sides. Drain on paper towels and sprinkle lightly with salt.

Ladle the hot soup into warmed shallow soup bowls and divide the garnishes among them.

A soup full of authentic Tex-Mex tastes. Adding the corn tortillas in the initial sautéing boosts the flavor of the broth, as well as adding body, and the soup is served with crisp corn tortilla strips and an assortment of colorful garnishes. Dean Fearing, the able chef who created it, says this soup has become a "signature dish" of the Mansion on Turtle Creek in Dallas. It has incredibly good flavor and can be a luncheon all by itself.

Chilled Pumpkin Soup

Makes about 1½ quarts; serves 6–8

2½-to-3-pound pumpkin
1 tablespoon butter
1 tablespoon vegetable oil
10–12 thin, peeled slices fresh ginger (about 1 ounce)
¼ teaspoon freshly grated nutmeg
5 cups Chicken Stock, page 166
1 cup plain yogurt
½ cup sour cream
Half-and-half, optional
3 pieces crystallized ginger, slivered

Quarter the pumpkin and cut out the stem end. Discard the seeds and fibers and peel off the skin with a swivel-bladed vegetable peeler. Cut the pumpkin into 1-inch pieces.

Heat the butter and vegetable oil in a large saucepan. Add the pumpkin, ginger slices and nutmeg and cook, stirring, for 3 minutes. Pour in 4 cups of the chicken stock and bring the mixture to a boil. Reduce the heat and simmer, partially covered, until the pumpkin is soft, 20 to 30 minutes.

Puree the soup in a food processor and transfer it to a large bowl. Whisk in the yogurt and sour cream and stir until the soup is smooth. Let it cool to room temperature; then cover the bowl and chill thoroughly.

At serving time, stir the soup with a whisk and adjust the consistency by stirring in some of the remaining chicken stock or some half-and-half. Serve cold, sprinkled with the crystallized ginger.

A recipe from the inventive menu at Atwater's in Portland, Oregon. Bill Geary, the chef, warns that harder pumpkins will absorb more of the stock than soft ones, so the yield will vary. It is also important to adjust the consistency of the soup, after it has chilled and the natural gelatin has thickened, by whisking in stock or half-and-half to achieve a smooth, creamy texture.

Silhouetted against the Dallas night sky, the Mansion on Turtle Creek, former home of a Texas cotton baron, has lost nothing of its splendor. Massed in the late-afternoon sunlight, brilliant orange pumpkins seem already lit from within.

Watercress and Potato Soup

Serves 8

1¾ cups chopped onions
¼ cup unsalted butter
2 cups coarsely chopped raw potatoes
5 cups Chicken Stock, page 166
½ teaspoon white pepper
1 teaspoon salt
4 cups chopped watercress leaves
  and stems, firmly packed
1 cup crème fraîche, sour cream or lightly whipped cream

Sauté the onions in the butter for 10 minutes, or until they are translucent. Add the potatoes, chicken stock, pepper and salt and bring to a boil.

Reduce the heat and simmer for 15 minutes, or until the potatoes are soft. Add the watercress and simmer for 5 more minutes.

Pour the soup into a blender or food processor and puree. Then pour the puree, through a strainer, back into the soup pot. Reheat the soup.

Serve each portion with 2 tablespoons of the cream you have selected.

A delicious and delicate version of the country French classic, as served by Margaret Fox in her tiny Café Beaujolais, housed in a Victorian clapboard cottage in Mendocino, California.

Daisies and veggies can claim equal prominence on a restaurant shopping list. Displayed in baskets or in crystal vases, flowers adorn nooks, crannies, pedestals and center-pieces—and a blossom can even turn up floating in the soup.

Red Pepper Soup

Serves 6 (small portions); makes 4 cups

6 large perfect red bell peppers
4 tablespoons butter
2 onions, finely chopped
3 cups Chicken Stock, page 166
Salt and pepper
2 teaspoons vinegar
12 fresh basil leaves, cut crosswise into thin strips,
   or substitute fresh marjoram, oregano or cilantro
½ cup crème fraîche

Remove the stems and seeds from the peppers and cut them into fairly small pieces.

Heat the butter and sauté the onions for 3 or 4 minutes until translucent. Add the cut-up peppers and the chicken stock. Simmer slowly, uncovered, for about 15 minutes until the peppers are tender but still brightly colored. Season with salt and pepper and a touch of vinegar.

Puree the soup in a food processor and chill overnight to allow the flavor to develop fully. Serve in small bowls, each garnished with shredded fresh herbs and a small spoonful of crème fraîche.

When Lewis Carroll sang the praises of "Soup of the evening, beautiful soup," he must surely have had Joyce Goldstein's Red Pepper Soup in mind. As served in her Square One restaurant in San Francisco, it makes a brilliant presentation with its vivid scarlet contrasted with shredded fresh green basil leaves and the stark whiteness of the crème fraîche. It also tastes glorious and is simplicity itself to make.

Cream of Leek and Shrimp Soup

Makes about 2 quarts; serves 6–10

6 cups Chicken Stock, page 166
1½ pounds medium-size shrimp, in their shells,
    26–30 per pound
½ cup (2½ ounces) prosciutto fat or ham fat, chopped
1½ tablespoons butter
4 cups chopped leeks, white and pale green part only
1 cup chopped carrots
1 cup chopped shallots
5 sprigs fresh thyme or 2 teaspoons dried
1 bay leaf
Stems from 1 bunch parsley
2 cups dry white wine
2 cups heavy cream
1 leek, white and pale green part only,
    cut into 1-inch-long julienne
Salt and freshly ground pepper

Bring the chicken stock to a boil. Add the shrimp and return to the boil. Remove the pan from the heat, cover and let rest for 1 minute. Remove the shrimp with a slotted spoon and let them cool; reserve the broth. Remove and reserve the shrimp shells. Cut the shrimp in half, lengthwise, deveining as needed, then set them aside, covered.

Combine the prosciutto fat and the butter in a large saucepan. Cook over moderate heat to render the fat, stirring occasionally, for 10 minutes. Add the shrimp shells and the chopped leeks, carrots and shallots. Cook for 5 minutes, stirring. Add the thyme, bay leaf, parsley stems and white wine and cook over high heat until the wine is reduced by half. Add the reserved chicken-shrimp broth. Bring to a boil, reduce the heat and simmer, partially covered, for 45 minutes. Remove the thyme sprigs and bay leaf.

While the soup is simmering, reduce and thicken the cream by cooking it over high heat for about 7 minutes.

Blanch the julienned leek in boiling salted water for 1 to 2 minutes, until tender. Refresh under cold water, drain and dry.

Puree the soup in a food processor and, for a silken texture, push it through a sieve. Discard the solids and return the soup to the pan. Add the reduced cream and salt and pepper to taste, and reheat.

Divide the shrimp among 6 soup bowls and pour in the hot soup. Garnish with the julienned leek.

A recipe from Chef Sandy D'Amato of John Byron's Restaurant in Milwaukee, this rich and satisfying soup is perfect with hot crusty bread and butter on a cold day. The combination of sherry and lemon juice in the soup opposite is a favorite of Chef Michael Roberts (above) of Trumps in Los Angeles, the recipe's originator.

Spooning crème fraîche in lines across the smoky soup makes possible the feathering that is a popular decorative technique in the new American cooking.

Black Bean Soup

Makes about 1½ quarts; serves 6–8

1½ cups dried black beans
6 cups Chicken Stock, page 166
½ pound smoked ham hocks
1½ tablespoons butter
¼ cup chopped carrot
¼ cup chopped celery
1 cup chopped onion
3 cloves garlic, sliced
2 bay leaves
1 sprig fresh thyme
   or ½ teaspoon dried
½ cup dry sherry
¼ cup fresh lemon juice
Salt and freshly ground pepper
6 tablespoons crème fraîche,
   at room temperature
6 thin slices lemon
¼ cup finely chopped red onion
1 hard-cooked egg, finely chopped

Rinse the beans, pick them over and soak for 14 hours in sufficient cold water to cover.

Combine the chicken stock and the ham hocks in a saucepan. Simmer over low heat, partially covered, for about 2 hours, or until the stock has a smoky flavor. Degrease, if necessary.

Heat the butter in a large saucepan over moderate heat. Add the carrot, celery and onion and cook, stirring occasionally, about 5 minutes. Add the garlic and stir for 1 minute. Add the drained soaked beans and 4 cups of the chicken stock; reserve any that remains. Add the bay leaves and the thyme. Bring to a boil, stirring occasionally. Reduce the heat and simmer, partially covered, until the beans are tender, about 1½ hours. Add the sherry and lemon juice and simmer for 5 more minutes.

Discard the bay leaves and thyme sprig and puree the soup in a food processor; then force it through a sieve. Return the soup to the pot and reheat over very low heat, stirring frequently. Thin with some of the reserved stock, if needed, so that the soup has a creamy consistency. Season to taste with salt and pepper.

To decorate the soup with the crème fraîche, the cream and soup must have the same consistency. If the cream is too thick, place it in a small bowl and set it in a larger bowl of warm water for a minute or two; stir it once or twice. Ladle the soup into 6 warmed shallow bowls. Using 1 tablespoon of crème fraîche for each bowl, spoon the cream in 3 evenly spaced stripes across the soup. Use the tip of a paring knife to feather the cream. Dip the tip into the cream and pull it outward on a 45-degree angle, every quarter inch or so, along both sides of each stripe. Pass the lemon slices, red onion and chopped egg in separate bowls for individual garnishing.

Bistro Salad

Serves 2

8 leaves of baby red leaf lettuce
4 leaves of bibb or Boston lettuce
1 head of Belgian endive
½ red bell pepper, julienned
¼ cup walnut oil
1 tablespoon fresh lemon juice
Salt and freshly ground pepper
8 walnut halves, coarsely chopped
2 tablespoons blue cheese, crumbled

Wash and dry the lettuces and tear them into bite-sized pieces. Combine them with the red pepper, the walnut oil, lemon juice and salt and pepper to taste. Toss well and divide between 2 chilled plates. Sprinkle the salads with walnuts and blue cheese.

How could we not include a dish with this name? It has other virtues as well and comes to us from Michael Foley of Printer's Row in Chicago. Use a local blue cheese, as he does, if you can find a good one.

Autumn Salad

Serves 4 as part of an appetizer

1 large carrot, peeled
1 leek, white part only, trimmed and washed
1 bulb fennel, branches and tough outer leaves removed
1 bunch chives, snipped
2 tablespoons champagne vinegar
4 tablespoons olive oil
Salt and freshly ground pepper

Cut the carrot and leek into 2-inch matchsticks. Cut the fennel bulb in half, lengthwise, and slice it across the grain to make crescent shapes.

Bring a large pot of salted water to a boil and blanch each vegetable separately for 15 seconds. Plunge them into a large pan of ice water, to retain their color. Drain and dry the vegetables and place them in a salad bowl.

Toss the vegetables with the chives, vinegar and oil and season to taste with salt and pepper.

This salad can be served alone or, as it commonly is at the Fifth Avenue Grill in New York City, as a component of Grilled Shrimp with Tomato-Dill Butter, page 40. It is one of the increasing group of salads that does not sport a single leaf of that traditional ingredient—lettuce.

Roast Pepper Salad with Olives and Walnut Oil

Serves 4 as an appetizer
Serves 12–15 as an hors d'oeuvre

4 red bell peppers
4 green bell peppers
2 yellow bell peppers
1 small onion
¾ cup pitted Provençal olives,
** or other Mediterranean olives**
** with low astringency**
3 tablespoons French walnut oil
½ teaspoon red wine vinegar
½ teaspoon fresh lemon juice
Salt and freshly ground pepper
4 sprigs Italian parsley

Roast and peel the peppers, following the method given on page 169. Cut them into strips ¼ inch wide by 2 inches long, and place them in a bowl.

Cut the onion into ¼-inch dice. It should be cleanly cut by hand, with a very sharp knife, and not bruised in a food processor or by chopping. Add it to the peppers.

Chop the olives into ¼-inch pieces and add them to the bowl. Toss the mixture gently.

Add the walnut oil, vinegar and lemon juice and salt and pepper to taste. Mix carefully, but well.

Let the salad mellow for at least an hour, unrefrigerated, in a cool place. It can be refrigerated for several days, but check the seasoning before serving; it may need another drop of lemon juice. Serve garnished with sprigs of parsley.

To quote Chef Leslie Revsin, who created this salad at the Metropolis restaurant in New York, "This is delicious by itself or as part of an antipasto—with marinated goat cheese or tiny fried quail. Wrap thin slices of rare grilled or roast filet mignon around small spoonfuls of salad and it becomes finger food." The first woman to break the all-male ranks in top-class American hotel kitchens when she became fish chef at the Waldorf Astoria a decade or so ago, Chef Revsin has acquired a reputation for really interesting food which brings folk flocking to the restaurants where she cooks.

Warm Potato Salad

Serves 8 as part of an appetizer

1½ pounds small red new potatoes
Salt
3 large shallots, thinly sliced and fluffed
    into rings
3 tablespoons chopped Italian parsley
⅓ cup finely chopped red bell pepper
⅓ cup finely chopped yellow
    bell pepper
¼ cup extra-virgin olive oil
2 tablespoons red wine vinegar
Freshly ground pepper

Simmer the potatoes, covered, in a large saucepan of lightly salted water for 20 to 25 minutes, or until they are tender.

Drain the potatoes, and while they are still warm, slice them into ¼-inch-thick rounds. Place them in a large bowl with the shallots, parsley and peppers.

Combine the olive oil and vinegar with salt and pepper to taste. Pour over the potatoes and mix gently, to avoid mashing the potatoes.

Serve this salad with Lamb Sausage with Watercress (page 146) as Chef Alfred Portale does at the Gotham Bar and Grill in New York City. It also goes well with any sausage.

Fall Greens with Smoked Chicken, Watercress and Pears, with Mustard-Herb Vinaigrette

Serves 4–6
Preheat the oven to 350 degrees

1 tablespoon butter
⅓ cup walnuts, cut into small pieces
½ small red onion, thinly sliced

Mustard-Herb Vinaigrette:

1 tablespoon Dijon mustard
¼ teaspoon salt
¼ teaspoon pepper
2 tablespoons tarragon vinegar
¼ teaspoon finely chopped garlic
½ teaspoon finely chopped shallot
1 tablespoon finely chopped
    basil, thyme or tarragon
½ cup mild vegetable oil
2–3 teaspoons fresh lemon juice

2 bunches watercress, trimmed
1 head Boston or butter lettuce
1 small head radicchio
1 cup thin strips of smoked chicken,
    about 5 ounces
½ large or 1 small Asian pear, if
    available, cored and thinly sliced
½ Comice, Bartlett or Bosc pear,
    cored and thinly sliced
4–6 pickled crab apples

Place the butter in a small pan and melt in the preheated oven. When it foams, stir in the walnuts and bake, stirring once or twice, for 10 to 12 minutes, until they are crisp. Spread them on paper towels to cool and drain.

Place the red onion slices in a small bowl with ice cubes. Cover with cold water and set aside.

Combine the mustard, salt, pepper, vinegar, garlic, shallot, and one of the herbs and mix well. Beat in the oil, a little at a time, and add lemon juice to taste. Set the dressing aside.

Wash and dry the salad greens. Reserve 6 sprigs of the watercress. Tear the lettuces into small pieces and combine them in a large bowl with the chicken, pears and two-thirds of the walnuts. Gradually add dressing to taste while tossing.

Distribute the salad equally on 4 to 6 plates. Sprinkle the remaining walnuts on top. Drain and dry the onion slices and strew over each salad. Garnish with the crab apples and watercress sprigs.

NOTE: Juicy, crisp, lightly sweet Asian pears are available in specialty markets during late fall and winter. If you cannot find them, use a whole American pear.

This festive, colorful salad makes a bright, light first course.

The salad described above and pictured at left comes from Chef Kathy Pavletich Casey (right), of Fullers in the Seattle Sheraton, where her cooking draws such crowds that even hotel guests must make reservations.

Lentil Salad

Serves 4–6

1 quart water
1 teaspoon salt
2 cups red lentils
¼ cup olive oil
¼ cup vegetable oil
2–3 tablespoons red wine vinegar
1 tablespoon Dijon mustard
2 teaspoons finely chopped garlic
½ teaspoon freshly ground black pepper
2 tablespoons finely chopped green bell pepper
2 tablespoons finely chopped red bell pepper
1 stalk celery, finely chopped
3 scallions, finely chopped
¼ cup sliced California olives

Bring the water and ½ teaspoon of the salt to a rolling boil. Add the lentils and simmer for 5 minutes. Remove the pan from the heat and allow the lentils to stand about 5 minutes, or until they begin to soften. Drain them well and transfer to a large bowl.

Whisk the oils, vinegar, mustard, garlic, pepper and remaining salt in a small bowl until they are well mixed. Pour over the lentils and toss thoroughly.

Stir in the vegetables and the olives and allow the flavors to develop for 30 minutes before serving. The salad should be served at room temperature.

A tasty, homespun salad from Mick's, part of the Peasant Restaurants in Atlanta, is flanked by two of today's most popular salad ingredients: radicchio and flavored vinegars.

Sliced Summer Fruits with Mango Puree

Serves 4

1 mango
2 tablespoons fresh lemon juice
Pinch of cayenne pepper
½ small papaya, peeled, seeded and sliced into thin wedges
¼ cantaloupe or honeydew melon, peeled, seeded and sliced into thin wedges
8 strawberries, hulled
¾ cup halved, pitted cherries (about ½ pound)
¼ grapefruit, peeled and sectioned
1 peach, peeled, pitted and sliced into wedges
2 plums, pitted and sliced
⅓ cup pecans (1 ounce)
4 sprigs fresh mint

Peel and chop the mango. Press it through a sieve to puree and remove the tough fibers. Place it in a small stainless steel or enamel saucepan and bring to a boil. Remove the pan from the heat and stir in the lemon juice and cayenne. Chill.

Divide the puree among 4 large serving plates. Arrange the fruit attractively on the plates and garnish with pecans and mint sprigs.

Above, a refreshing recipe from The Four Seasons' famous Spa Cuisine menu. If you want to be really serious, accompany it with a glass of sparkling non-alcoholic white wine.

Great-Grandmother's Wild Greens

Serves 6

1 medium-size onion, finely chopped
1 bunch each collard greens,
　　mustard greens and turnip greens
2 medium-size tomatoes, peeled,
　　seeded and chopped
2 cloves garlic, sliced
1¼ teaspoons coarse salt
½ teaspoon freshly ground
　　black pepper
1 cup vegetable oil
½ teaspoon fresh lemon juice
⅓ cup white wine vinegar
2 teaspoons dry mustard
2 tablespoons sugar
½ teaspoon Worcestershire sauce
½ teaspoon Tabasco

Put the onion in a small bowl with an ice cube and cold water, and let it soak for 20 minutes, to remove its "bite."

Remove the stems from the greens, wash and dry the leaves, and tear them into bite-sized pieces. Place the greens on 6 chilled salad plates.

Drain the onion and pat it dry. Toss it with the chopped tomatoes and spoon the mixture onto the greens.

Place the garlic, salt, pepper and 2 tablespoons of the oil in the container of a blender or food processor. Process until a paste is formed. Add the lemon juice, vinegar, mustard, sugar, Worcestershire and Tabasco and blend until smooth. With the motor running, add the remaining oil in a steady stream.

Drizzle the dressing over the greens and serve.

This evocatively titled recipe takes a step back in time, yet has a thoroughly modern flavor. It comes from the American Restaurant in Kansas City's Crown Center, where Chef Kenneth Dunn specializes in truly American regional dishes, and Richard King, the restaurant's owner, says that of all the recipes on the menu, this one is an absolute "must."

Smoked Salmon Salad

Serves 6

Dressing:

2 tablespoons red wine vinegar
1 tablespoon fresh lemon juice
1 tablespoon Dijon mustard
½ cup olive oil
½ teaspoon coarse salt
½ teaspoon freshly ground pepper

12 small, freshly cooked
　　new potatoes, sliced
1 small green pepper, julienned
3 tablespoons each finely chopped
　　shallots, parsley and chives
1 bunch leaf lettuce,
　　in bite-sized pieces
1 head radicchio, in bite-sized pieces
⅓ pound smoked salmon, cut in strips
3–6 tablespoons crème fraîche
3–6 tablespoons salmon roe
1 tablespoon chopped lovage, optional

Combine the dressing ingredients in a jar and shake thoroughly.

Put the potatoes, green pepper, shallots, and 2 tablespoons each of the parsley and chives in a bowl and toss gently with two-thirds of the dressing.

Toss the leaf lettuce and radicchio with the remaining dressing and transfer to 6 chilled plates. Arrange the potatoes on the salad and divide the salmon strips among the plates. Add a mound of crème fraîche to each salad, and top with a spoonful of salmon roe. Sprinkle with the remaining parsley, chives and the optional lovage.

Smoked salmon is always one of the most satisfactory of ingredients—delicate, colorful, full of flavor and easy to work with—and this salad uses it to perfection. It was devised by Chef Alfred Portale of the Gotham Bar and Grill in New York, who is seen enjoying it at right.

Some of the salads offered for our sampling have their origins in time-honored recipes; others are as new as this morning's brilliant thought. Why not mingle endives, red peppers and walnuts in a lime dressing on a black scallop shell? Why not indeed! It's a time for experimenting—and enjoying the results.

Braised Rapini

Serves 4–6

2 pounds rapini (broccoli rabe)
¼ cup olive oil
6–10 garlic cloves, peeled and crushed

Trim and discard the tough lower stems of the rapini, then chop it coarsely, crosswise.

Heat the olive oil in a large skillet over low heat. Add the garlic cloves and cook slowly, until they are golden. Add the rapini to the pan and stir to mix it with the oil and garlic. Raise the heat to moderate and cover the pan. Braise the greens until they wilt and are tender, about 10 to 15 minutes. Lift the cover and stir once or twice during the cooking; if the pan looks too dry, add a tablespoon or two of water.

Serve the rapini warm or at room temperature. It is delicious on bread.

Another recipe from Angeli, the starkly modern cafe-pizzeria in Los Angeles where Evan Kleiman offers her own interpretation of both plain and fancy food from the Italian countryside.

In the best possible diet every element would equal the sweet young carrot pulled from the soft earth, rinsed under the garden hose and eaten on the spot. To come close to this ideal, chefs use only the freshest vegetables—and often their blossoms, too.

Artichokes Alla Romana

Serves 8
Preheat the oven to 375 degrees

8 artichokes, about 8 ounces each
1 cup parsley
6 large cloves garlic, peeled
5 tablespoons anchovy fillets,
  oil included
½ cup lemon juice
½ cup dry white wine
3 cups olive oil
3 cups water
Salt to taste

Hold the artichoke on its side and, with a sharp knife, trim the leaves away as close to the bottom as possible, turning the artichoke as you work. Leave the stem intact. Cut the leaves off the top, just above the artichoke bottom. Using a teaspoon, scoop out the choke and discard it. Trim away the remaining leaves and pieces, leaving the bottom. Pare any tough outside fibers from the stem.

Chop the parsley, garlic and anchovies in a food processor. Add the lemon juice, wine, olive oil, water and salt to taste. Process briefly to combine.

Arrange the artichokes in a single layer in a heatproof baking dish. Pour the marinade over the artichokes, making sure the stems are covered. Place the dish on high heat and bring to a boil. Cover and transfer the artichokes to the oven. Cook covered, turning and basting occasionally, for 45 to 60 minutes, or until the stems are tender.

Make these at least a day in advance of serving so that the flavors mellow.

At the Stanford Court (left), these are served slightly warmed or at room temperature; you can survey the San Francisco skyline as you savor each leaf

Warm Escarole Stuffed with Mozzarella and Roasted Peppers

Serves 6
Preheat the oven to 400 degrees

1 red bell pepper
⅛ teaspoon salt
Freshly ground pepper
8 tablespoons olive oil
1 teaspoon finely chopped garlic
1 tablespoon chopped fresh marjoram or thyme or
   2 tablespoons finely chopped fresh basil
16 large escarole leaves (dark outer leaves)
12 1-ounce slices whole-milk mozzarella

Grill the pepper directly in a gas flame or under a broiler until it is evenly charred. Wrap it in damp paper towels and let it stand 10 minutes. Scrape away all the skin and remove the ribs and seeds. Cut it into slivers, about 1 inch long. Combine with the salt, pepper to taste, 2 tablespoons of the olive oil, garlic and the herb you have selected.

Bring a large pot of salted water to a boil and add the escarole leaves. When the water returns to a boil, let them cook for a few seconds, just until the leaf bases are softened. Drain the leaves, then plunge them into ice water. Drain again and spread them flat, in a single layer, between paper towels.

Place 2 overlapping leaves on a work surface to make as large a rectangle as possible. Put a piece of cheese in the center; spoon a sixth of the pepper mixture onto the cheese, then cover with a second slice of cheese. Wrap the leaves tightly over the cheese, to make a compact package, and place the packet in a baking pan. Repeat 5 times. You will have a few extra leaves for patching, if needed.

Bake the packages in the preheated oven for 5 minutes, or until the cheese begins to melt.

Place the packages on individual serving plates, drizzle a tablespoon of oil over each, sprinkle with a little fresh pepper and serve immediately.

Extremely tasty, bright-green packets with a surprise inside from Daniel Malzhan, the inventive chef at San Francisco's Café Americain.

Salmon Baked in Parchment With Herbs and Vegetables

Serves 4
Preheat the oven to 375 degrees

1 stalk celery, peeled
1 medium-size carrot, peeled
1 medium-size leek, white and tender green
Vegetable oil
8 salmon fillets (about 3 ounces each)
4 teaspoons dry white wine
4 teaspoons fresh lemon juice
4 teaspoons bottled clam juice
1 medium-size tomato, peeled, seeded and chopped
8 sprigs of fresh tarragon or a pinch of dried
1 tablespoon minced fresh chervil or parsley
Freshly ground pepper

Cut the celery, carrot and leek into thin julienne strips and blanch them, until crisp-tender, in a pot of boiling water. Drain and rinse under cold running water; drain and dry on paper towels.

Cut 4 sheets of parchment into heart shapes, each 20 inches wide. Brush lightly with oil. Spread one-fourth of the vegetables over half of each parchment heart. Place 2 salmon fillets on each bed of vegetables.

Combine the wine, lemon juice and clam juice in a bowl. Pour 1 tablespoon of the mixture over each portion of fish.

Sprinkle about 1 tablespoon of chopped tomato over each. Chop 4 of the tarragon sprigs and combine with the chervil and sprinkle evenly over each portion. Season with pepper to taste and top with a sprig of tarragon.

Fold the other half of the heart over the salmon and seal the papillotes with a series of tight, overlapping folds. Place them on a large baking sheet and bake in the center of the preheated oven for 10 minutes, or until the bags are puffed up. Serve at once, letting each guest cut the papillote open at the table.

Tim Ryan of the American Bounty in Hyde Park, New York, developed this recipe; it is really excellent diet food, fragrant with herbs.

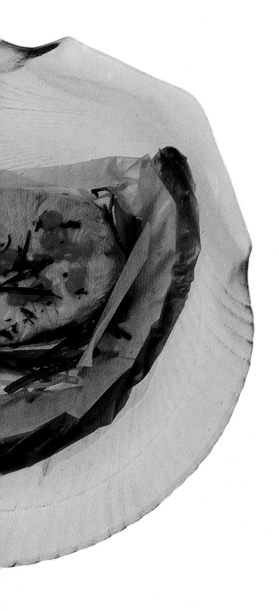

Top, a brief lull before the crowds at Café Americain's stylishly simple bar; below, the recipe at right unwraps its aromatic secret.

Lamb Sausage with Watercress

Serves 8 as an appetizer

1¼ pounds boneless lamb shoulder,
   trimmed
1 pound boneless fatty pork shoulder
2½ teaspoons salt
½ teaspoon freshly ground
   white pepper
¼ teaspoon sugar
¼ teaspoon each finely chopped
   fresh rosemary, thyme, and sage
¼ teaspoon finely chopped garlic
2 tablespoons finely chopped
   Italian parsley
Natural hog casings, optional
1 bunch watercress, stems trimmed
1 teaspoon red wine vinegar
1 tablespoon extra-virgin olive oil

Cut the lamb and pork into 2-inch cubes and chill in the freezer for about 15 minutes. Place the meat in the container of a food processor and chop to a medium-coarse consistency by pulsing 12 to 15 times. Transfer the meat to a bowl, add all of the seasonings and mix thoroughly.

Use a sausage stuffer, according to the manufacturer's instructions, to make sausages in the casings. Or scoop up the meat, ¼ cup at a time, and form it into 16 patties, about 3 inches in diameter.

Either grill the sausages for about 5 minutes on each side, or sauté them in a heavy skillet filmed with olive oil. Sear the meat quickly on each side over moderately high heat. Reduce the heat to moderately low and cook for about 5 minutes on the first side, then 3 minutes on the second. The meat will be slightly pink.

Toss the watercress with the vinegar and oil and divide it among 8 plates. Arrange 2 sausages on each plate and serve with the Warm Potato Salad on page 136.

From Chef Alfred Portale at the Gotham Bar & Grill in New York, a typical European-style bistro known and loved by a wide range of people for its varied, eclectic menu.

Lobster Tortelloni

Serves 6 as an appetizer

Filling:

4 ounces cooked lobster meat
1 ounce shelled uncooked shrimp
⅓ cup ricotta cheese
1 teaspoon finely chopped fresh chives
¾ teaspoon finely chopped
   fresh chervil or parsley
1½ teaspoons fish-lobster base
   or bottled clam juice
½ teaspoon coarse salt
½ teaspoon cognac
½ large egg yolk, beaten
White pepper to taste

Pasta dough:

1½ cups flour
2 large eggs, beaten
½ teaspoon salt
2½ teaspoons olive oil
2½ teaspoons lukewarm water
3 tablespoons butter, melted

Sauce:

1 cup heavy cream
3 tablespoons fish-lobster base
1 teaspoon cognac
Salt and white pepper to taste
1 tablespoon finely chopped chives

Sharp contrasts in the wrapping department: at left, a chicken enclosed in moist grape leaves and a traditional layer of baked mud; right, a spicy filling done up in a frilly country cap of delicate filo pastry.

Place the lobster and shrimp in the container of a food processor and pulse rapidly about 6 times, until the fish is finely chopped, but not pureed. Add the remaining filling ingredients and pulse briefly to combine them. Transfer the mixture to a bowl, cover and refrigerate.

To make the pasta dough, combine all of the ingredients, except the butter, by hand or in a processor. Work them together until they form a slightly sticky ball. Knead the dough by hand on a lightly floured surface for 7 to 10 minutes, or until the dough is smooth and elastic. Divide the dough in half and cover one half with plastic wrap while you roll out the other. Roll the dough by hand, or with a pasta machine, until it is thin but not quite transparent. Repeat with the remaining dough.

Cut the dough into circles, using a 2½-inch biscuit cutter or a small drinking glass. Put a scant teaspoon of the filling in the center of each circle and fold it in half so that the bottom edge comes just below the top. Press to seal the edges well, then bend the pasta around your finger, pinching the 2 points of the tortelloni together to form a ring. Make sure the seal is tight.

Bring a large pot of salted water to a rapid boil. Add the tortelloni and let the water return to a boil. Stir once and cook the pasta for 3 to 5 minutes, or until it is "al dente." Remove the tortelloni to a warmed bowl, using a slotted spoon. Coat them with the melted butter and keep warm.

To make the sauce, combine the cream and fish-lobster base in a small non-corrodible saucepan. Reduce the mixture, over moderately high heat, to about ¾ cup, to thicken the cream. Stir in the cognac, while the cream is still simmering, and add salt and pepper to taste. Mix the sauce with the buttered tortelloni and divide among 6 warm serving plates. Sprinkle with chives and serve immediately.

These days seafood is a popular item on Midwestern as well as East and West Coast menus. This excellent recipe is from Fedora Café and Bar in Kansas City, Missouri.

At Arcadia (left), Anne Rosenzweig has created a small restaurant of extra-ordinary warmth and charm, dedicated to the comfort of every guest, from the furnishings to the food. As you go in, warm and luscious smells emanate from the kitchen—and you are never disappointed.

Coconut Tuiles

Makes 12 to 15 5-inch cookies
Preheat the oven to 350 degrees

3–5 tablespoons clarified butter, melted
½ cup sugar
2 large eggs
¼ cup flour
1¾ cups shredded, unsweetened
   coconut, loosely packed
   (about 3½ ounces)

Line several cookie sheets with parchment paper and lightly brush with clarified butter. Or, butter the sheets and dust them with flour. Rap them firmly, to knock off any excess flour. Mark three 5-inch circles on each sheet.

Whisk the sugar and eggs together. Add the flour and continue to whisk until they are well combined. Stir in 2 tablespoons of the butter and the coconut.

Spread rounded tablespoonfuls of the batter evenly in the traced circles. The batter should be very thinly spread so that the tuiles are as delicate as possible.

Bake the tuiles for 5 to 8 minutes, until they are golden brown around the edges and pale in the center. Remove the cookies with a thin metal spatula, using a deft sliding motion. Immediately mold the tuiles over the bottoms of coffee cups. When they have cooled and hardened, remove them and fill with Frozen Mango Mousse.

Raspberry-Strawberry Puree

Makes about 2 cups

1 pint fresh raspberries
1 pint fresh strawberries, hulled
2 tablespoons Framboise

Press the raspberries through a sieve, to remove the seeds. Combine the berries, and Framboise in a food processor and puree.

In the photograph above, these three recipes are combined, Arcadia-style, by ladling a thin layer of puree on each plate, setting a mousse-filled tuile in the center and decorating it with a mint sprig or fresh fruit.

Frozen Mango Mousse in Coconut Tuiles with a Raspberry-Strawberry Puree

Serves 6

3 very ripe mangos
3 tablespoons fresh lime juice
1 tablespoon Triple Sec
⅓ cup superfine sugar
2 egg whites
¾ cup heavy cream

Peel the mangos and cut the flesh from the pits. Chop it roughly and puree in a food processor or food mill. There should be approximately 2 cups. Stir in the lime juice, Triple Sec and sugar.

Beat the egg whites until they are stiff. Beat the cream until soft peaks form. Fold the whites gently into the puree and then fold in the whipped cream.

Transfer the mixture to a chilled ice cream machine canister and freeze it according to the manufacturer's directions.

Anne Rosenzweig (who is pictured on the Contents page) was an anthropologist before she became a chef and co-owner of a New York restaurant—and her perceptive, subtle combinations of food make her one of the most interesting cooks (and best recipe writers) at work today.

Cinnamon Ice Cream

Makes 1 quart

1¼ cups half-and-half
2½ cups heavy cream
1 cup less 1 tablespoon sugar
1 stick cinnamon
½ teaspoon ground cinnamon
6 egg yolks

Heat the half-and-half, cream, sugar and both kinds of cinnamon in a non-corrodible saucepan. Cook on the lowest heat for about 15 minutes; maintain the temperature below boiling. Check to be sure the cinnamon taste remains subtle. This flavor becomes more obvious with freezing.

Lightly whisk the egg yolks and gradually add some of the cream mixture, to warm them. Add the warmed yolks to the cream and cook over low heat, stirring constantly, until the custard coats a spoon. Strain into a container and put in the cinnamon stick if you want the flavor more pronounced. Chill thoroughly and remove it.

Freeze in an ice cream machine, according to the manufacturer's instructions.

A dessert from Chez Panisse, the wonderful Berkeley bistro where Alice Waters reigns supreme. Was it only a decade ago that this attractive young amateur went to France and came back determined to cook only the freshest and best foods and combine them in simply splendid new ways? Her vision has been a seminal influence on the new American cooking.

Turtle Cay Bananas with Passion Fruit Sauce

Serves 4

4 bananas
¼ cup brown sugar
¼ cup dark rum
1 teaspoon finely chopped fresh ginger
⅛ teaspoon salt
4–6 passion fruit
¼–⅓ cup simple syrup
4 tablespoons butter

Peel and slice the bananas lengthwise. Combine the sugar, 2 tablespoons of the rum, the ginger and half the salt in a large flat dish. Stir to dissolve the sugar. Arrange the bananas in the dish and marinate 1 hour, turning occasionally.

Cut the passion fruit in half and scrape the pulp into a bowl. Stir in ¼ cup of the simple syrup and the remaining salt. Taste and adjust the sweetness, if needed.

Heat 2 tablespoons of the butter in a skillet and add the bananas, flat side down. Pour in the marinade and cook on low heat for 5 minutes. Add the remaining rum to the bananas, raise the heat and ignite the liquid. Shake the pan and when the flames from the rum are gone, swirl in the remaining butter.

Arrange the bananas on warm plates and pour their juices and the passion fruit sauce over them.

This is what Jeremiah Tower, its creator, calls "new Florida cuisine."

Feast your eyes on Chaya's laden dessert table, then dream of caging ice cream in spun caramel. It's sweet to fantasize.

Coconut Ice

Makes about 1½ quarts

1¼ cups sugar
1½ cups water
2 cans (12–14 ounces each) unsweetened coconut milk
6 large egg whites (¾ cup)
⅛ teaspoon salt

Combine the sugar and water in a small saucepan over moderate heat. Bring the mixture to a boil, stirring frequently to dissolve the sugar. Let it cool to room temperature.

Whisk the coconut milk in a large mixing bowl until smooth. Stir in the cooled sugar syrup, transfer to an ice cream freezer and freeze according to the manufacturer's directions. When the mixture is slushy, beat the egg whites with the salt until stiff peaks form. Fold the whites into the icy mixture and freeze until firm.

The coconut ice can also be still-frozen. Make your freezer as cold as possible before you start. Turn the mixture into a metal pan and place it in the freezer. Whisk every 20 minutes or so, until it becomes slushy. Beat the egg whites and salt until stiff peaks form. Fold into the coconut ice and freeze until firm.

Individual Hazelnut Tarts with Semi-Sweet Fresh Cream

Serves 6
Preheat the oven to 350 degrees

Tart shells:

¼ cup sugar
4 ounces butter, at room temperature
1 large egg, beaten
1½ cups flour
¼ teaspoon vanilla extract

Filling:

3 large eggs, beaten
½ cup sugar
½ cup dark corn syrup
1½ tablespoons cider vinegar
1 tablespoon butter, melted and cooled
½ teaspoon vanilla extract
Pinch of salt
2 cups hazelnuts (about ¾ pound), toasted, peeled
   and coarsely chopped, see page 169

Cream:

1 cup heavy cream
½ teaspoon confectioners' sugar
⅛ teaspoon vanilla extract

To make the tart shells, cream the sugar and butter until they are fluffy. Add the egg and beat until the mixture is smooth and well blended. Add the flour and vanilla and mix well. The dough will be soft and slightly sticky. Divide it into 6 equal balls, cover with plastic wrap and let them rest in the refrigerator for 10 minutes.

Lightly flour a rolling pin and work surface and roll out each ball of dough into a 4½-inch circle. Lightly press the dough into 3½-inch tart pans and refrigerate, covered, for 1 hour or until the pastry is firm.

To make the filling, beat the eggs and sugar until they are well blended. Add the corn syrup, vinegar, butter, vanilla and salt and mix well. Stir in the hazelnuts.

Spoon the filling into the chilled tart shells; it should come to within ¼ inch of the top of the shells. Bake in the preheated oven for 15 to 20 minutes, until the center is set and the crust is golden brown.

Whip the cream until it forms soft peaks; then fold in the sugar and vanilla.

Serve the tarts warm, topped with a dollop of cream.

An invention of Chef Sandy D'Amato of John Byron's Restaurant in Milwaukee, these are nutty and rich and sticky and good—the kind of dessert that as children we used to long for, interpreted for adults.

Thin Apple Pancakes with Broiled Apple Slices and Apple Cider Ice Cream

Serves 6

Apple Pancakes:

½ cup flour
2 tablespoons sugar
½ teaspoon salt
1 egg
1 egg white
½ cup milk, at room temperature
½ cup dry sparkling apple cider,
    at room temperature
¼ cup clarified butter, melted

Broiled Apple Slices:

2–3 tart, green apples
2 cups dry sparkling apple cider
½ cup sugar
⅓ teaspoon cinnamon

To make the pancakes, sift the flour into a large bowl, make a well in the center and sprinkle the sugar and salt over the top.

Combine the other ingredients, beat lightly with a fork and pour into the well in the flour. Slowly and gradually, draw the dry ingredients into the liquid, little by little, using a whisk or a wooden spoon. Continue until all the ingredients are mixed and smooth. Let the batter stand for at least 1 hour. (You can refrigerate it, covered, overnight, if you do not add the butter. Bring it back to room temperature, then stir in the butter before making the pancakes.)

Heat a 5-inch non-stick skillet over moderately high heat, testing the temperature by flicking a drop of water on the surface. When the pan is at the right temperature, the water will splatter and dance.

Measure 1½ tablespoons batter into a small container and pour it all at once into the pan, swirling it around to make an even coating. The batter should sizzle as it is poured into the pan. Cook over moderately high heat for 1 minute, or until the pancake has a lacy look, with nicely browned edges. Run a spatula around them and flip the pancake, then cook for 30 seconds more. Set it on a plate and repeat the process, stirring the batter each time before measuring it. Stack the pancakes as you finish them; there should be 18 in all. (They may be made up to 24 hours ahead and stored at room temperature, wrapped in plastic.)

To make the apple slices, peel and core the apples, leaving them whole. Cut each across into ⅜-inch-thick rings, discarding the slices at the ends. There should be about 6 rings from each apple. Place them in a bowl, cover with the cider and macerate for 2 hours.

Preheat the broiler 30 minutes before serving time. Toss together the sugar and cinnamon. Pat the apples dry and dip one side of each slice in the sugar to coat it. Arrange the slices on a broiling pan, sugar side up, and broil 3 to 5 minutes, until the tops are caramelized and the slices are tender. They will not all take the same amount of time to caramelize, so watch carefully and remove the slices that are done and reposition the others to continue cooking. Reserve the slices until you are ready to assemble the dessert. (The caramel will lose its crispness after 30 minutes.)

To assemble the dessert, preheat the oven to 350 degrees and have 6 ovenproof dessert plates ready. Place a pancake on each plate, set 2 apple slices on each pancake and cover with 2 more pancakes. Place a third apple slice on top.

Place the filled plates in the oven for 3 to 5 minutes, just to warm the pancakes through. Remove them, place a small scoop of Apple Cider Ice Cream in the center of the crowning apple ring, and serve immediately.

Apple Cider Ice Cream

Makes about 1½ quarts

8 egg yolks
2 cups heavy cream
2 cups milk
1½ cups dry sparkling apple cider
1 cup sugar
2 large cinnamon sticks

Favored settings for elegant Bostonians: a table underneath the striking arches (left) at Seasons, in the heart of the Faneuil Hall Marketplace, or at Jasper's, a restaurant that flows from room to room, where each nook has its own ambiance, and the flowers (above) are always as superbly styled as the food.

Whisk the egg yolks lightly in a large bowl and set aside.

Scald the cream and milk in a large heavy saucepan and keep warm over low heat.

Combine the apple cider, sugar and cinnamon sticks in a non-corrodible saucepan. Cook over high heat until the mixture reduces and turns a dark amber color, 20 to 25 minutes. Remove the cinnamon sticks and immediately begin whisking the mixture into the warm cream and milk, incorporating about a third at a time. (Be careful—the cream will spatter and bubble up. But the caramelized cider *must* be poured into the cream as quickly as possible or it will continue to cook and burn in the pan.) When all the caramel has been whisked in, reheat the cream, stirring constantly, until the cider is completely incorporated.

Pour a quarter of the hot mixture into the egg yolks, whisking continuously, then pour it back into the saucepan and cook over low heat, stirring constantly with a wooden spoon until the mixture thickens enough to coat the back of the spoon. Strain the custard through a fine mesh strainer into a bowl. Whisk it a few times to release the heat, then refrigerate until thoroughly chilled.

Freeze the custard in an ice cream freezer according to the manufacturer's instructions.

"Every component of this beautifully composed dessert can be eaten separately," says its author, Nancy Silverton, the pastry chef at Maxwell's Plum in New York City. "But in this case, the whole is greater than the sum of its parts. The contrasts of warm and cold, chewy and creamy, crisp and soft make a very special combination." Try to use imported French "brut" cider throughout, as she does.

Goat Cheese Cake with Raspberries and Hazelnuts

Serves 10
Preheat the oven to 350 degrees

Cheesecake:

2 tablespoons softened butter
2½ pounds mild goat cheese,
    such as Goat Folks Farm
6 large eggs
2⅓ cups sifted confectioners' sugar
2 tablespoons cornstarch
1 cup sour cream

Hazelnut crust:

1 cup toasted and peeled hazelnuts,
    coarsely ground, see page 169
½ cup plus 1 tablespoon flour
7 tablespoons granulated sugar
7 tablespoons butter, softened
1 small egg

Raspberry sauce:

2 10-ounce packages frozen raspberries
    in light syrup, thawed
3 tablespoons superfine sugar

It's the end of the
day, and Jasper's chefs
take time for a joke.

Let the cheesecake ingredients stand at room temperature for 1 hour. Coat the insides of 2 10-inch cake pans with the butter. Line the bottoms with circles of kitchen parchment and set one pan aside for the crust. Cut a strip of parchment and line the inside of the other pan.

Crumble the goat cheese into a large mixing bowl and beat with a hand-held electric mixer just until smooth. Add the following ingredients in turn, beating just long enough to incorporate each one; don't overbeat or the cheese may separate. Beat in the eggs, 2 at a time. Add ½ cup of confectioners' sugar and the cornstarch and beat until smooth. Beat in the remaining sugar, ½ cup at a time, then the sour cream.

Pour the batter into the lined pan and place it in a larger pan. Add very hot tap water to the outer pan to come halfway up the sides of the cake pan. Bake the cake for about 20 minutes, just until the center has set and is no longer soupy when the pan is nudged gently. Remove the cheesecake from the water bath and cool to room temperature on a rack, still in its pan. Cover with aluminum foil and refrigerate for 12 hours.

To make the crust, preheat the oven to 375 degrees.

Combine the hazelnuts and flour in a small bowl. Beat the sugar and butter in a large bowl until fluffy. Beat in the egg, then stir in the hazelnut mixture. Press into the bottom of the reserved prepared pan, in an even layer, and bake until golden brown, 20 to 25 minutes. Cool the crust in the pan, set on a rack.

To make the sauce, puree the raspberries in the food processor, place a sieve over a bowl and force the puree through. Stir the superfine sugar into the puree until dissolved.

Remove the cheesecake in its pan from the refrigerator and place over a heated burner briefly to loosen the bottom (take care not to let it burn). Set a 12-inch round of cardboard, or a flat plate, over the top of the cake, hold them tightly together, and invert both onto a work surface, shaking to loosen the cake from the pan onto the cardboard. Peel off the parchment and discard it.

Run a knife around the edge of the cooled crust and invert the pan onto your hand. (If the crust does not fall out, heat the pan briefly over the burner and try again.) Remove the parchment and invert the crust over the bottom of the cheesecake.

Place a flat serving platter on top of the crust. Carefully and securely pick up the entire stack and turn it right side up. Remove the top cardboard or plate.

Cut the cake into wedges, using a knife with a thin, sharp, long blade, and serve with the raspberry sauce.

Created by Leslie Mackie, the pastry chef at Jasper's in Boston, this cheesecake is refreshingly new. The crunchy hazelnut crust stays that way, thanks to its careful, separate baking, and the slightly sweet raspberry sauce sets off the lightly salty flavor of the goat cheese admirably.

Glistening fruit takes
tempting guises—piled
on a plate, or swirled
on pastry crusts.

Armagnac Hazelnut Pudding

Serves 8–10

¾ cup Armagnac
4 egg yolks
⅔ cup sugar
8 tablespoons butter, melted
1½ cups heavy cream
1 cup hazelnuts (about 5 ounces), toasted,
  peeled and chopped, see page 169

In a small saucepan over high heat, reduce the Armagnac to ⅓ cup; it can ignite, so be cautious. Combine the egg yolks and sugar in the top of a double boiler and stir in the Armagnac. Place the pan over simmering water and beat the mixture until it is light and thickened, about 5 minutes. Stir in the butter and set aside to cool to room temperature.

Whip the cream until stiff and fold into the cooled egg yolk mixture with half of the chopped hazelnuts. Spoon into small individual serving dishes or into a large serving bowl. Chill until firm, about 2 hours, sprinkle with the remaining hazelnuts, and serve.

An exquisite dessert from Manhattan's Casual Quilted Giraffe. And, in his new bistro, chef-owner Barry Wine still takes care of every detail—even to designing the plates (above).

Double Dark Chocolate Cake with White Chocolate Sauce

Serves 8–12
Preheat the oven to 350 degrees

Cake:

1 cup heavy cream
10½ ounces semi-sweet chocolate, chopped in small pieces
2 ounces unsweetened chocolate, chopped in small pieces
5 eggs
⅓ cup sugar
1 teaspoon vanilla extract

Frosting:

4 ounces semi-sweet chocolate
5 tablespoons butter, softened
2 tablespoons bourbon
2 eggs, separated
1½ tablespoons sugar

Sauce:

5 ounces white chocolate, chopped in small pieces
1 cup heavy cream

A page to delight every chocolate fan: two superb recipes and a picture that celebrates the quintessence of chocolate.

To prepare the cake, cut a round of wax paper or parchment to fit the bottom of a 9-inch round cake pan. Butter the pan, fit in the paper, then butter it. Coat the pan with flour, tapping out the excess.

Bring the cream to a boil in a heavy 3-quart saucepan. Remove it from the heat and stir in both chocolates. Cover the pan and let it stand for 5 minutes. Stir the mixture until it is smooth. Set aside, uncovered.

Combine the eggs, sugar and vanilla in a large bowl. Set the bowl over simmering water and whisk the mixture constantly until it is hot, about 2 minutes. Remove the bowl from the heat and beat with an electric mixer on moderate, then high speed until the mixture has tripled in volume, cooled, and is as thick as a soft meringue, about 8 minutes.

With a whisk, stir one-third of the egg mixture into the chocolate. Gently fold in the remainder with a rubber spatula, blending until only a few chocolate streaks remain. Pour the batter into the cake pan and smooth the top. Place it in a larger pan and carefully pour in boiling water to reach halfway up the sides.

Bake in the center of the oven for 50 minutes, or until a toothpick inserted in the center comes out clean. Let the cake cool for 30 minutes in the water, then remove it and place on a rack to cool completely. When it is completely cooled, run a knife around the edge of the pan and invert onto a serving dish. Gently remove the paper.

To prepare the frosting, combine the chocolate and butter in the upper part of a large double boiler. Set over simmering water and stir occasionally until they are melted. Remove the pan from the heat and let the mixture cool for 10 minutes. Add the bourbon and stir; whisk in the egg yolks, one at a time.

Beat the egg whites to form soft peaks. Gradually add the sugar, beating until stiff peaks form, about 2 minutes. Fold one-quarter of this mixture into the chocolate and blend well. Fold in the remaining whites with a rubber spatula, blending until the whites are barely incorporated. Chill for at least 2 hours.

To prepare the sauce, place the white chocolate in the top part of a double boiler over simmering water. Stir until it is melted. Add the cream and stir for a minute. Cool to room temperature. (The sauce can be chilled, then warmed slightly to blend it, then cooled to room temperature for serving.)

To assemble the cake, scoop the frosting gently into a pastry tube fitted with a fairly wide (Number 4) star tube. Pipe the mixture over the top of the cake. You can chill the cake for as long as 2 days.

To serve the cake, let it reach room temperature, which will take about 3 hours. Stir the sauce, then pour a small pool onto each serving plate. Place a slice of cake on the sauce.

From Stephan Pyles, creative chef of Dallas's Routh Street Cafe.

Chocolate Mousse with Chocolate Butterfly Wings

Serves 8

8 ounces semi-sweet chocolate,
   cut into 16 pieces
1⅓ cups heavy cream
1 tablespoon Crème de Cacao
1½ teaspoons dark rum
4 large egg whites
½ cup sugar

Butterfly Wings:

4 ounces semi-sweet chocolate,
   cut into small pieces

Whipped cream

Place the chocolate in the container of a food processor and pulse 12 times to chop, then continue processing to make it fine. Heat ⅓ cup of the cream in a small saucepan. When it comes to a boil, pour it into the chopped chocolate and process until smooth. Add the Crème de Cacao and rum and pulse several times. Scrape the mixture into a mixing bowl and cool completely.

Whip the remaining cream in a chilled bowl until soft peaks form. Gently fold the cream into the cooled chocolate mixture until it is almost uniform in color, with just a few streaks apparent.

Combine the egg whites and sugar in a large bowl and set over a saucepan containing several inches of simmering water. Whisk the mixture constantly until it is lukewarm (about 100 degrees), for about 1 minute. Remove from the heat and continue whisking or beating the whites until soft peaks form, about 1 minute. Fold gently into the chocolate cream to blend thoroughly.

Divide the mousse among 8 ¾-cup bowls or ramekins. Refrigerate for at least 3 hours before serving.

To make the Butterfly Wings, melt the chocolate over barely simmering water until it is smooth, stirring often. Remove from the heat and let it cool briefly, until it is no longer as runny, about 5 minutes. Make a small parchment cone and cut a 1/16-inch opening. Cover a baking sheet with wax paper or parchment. Slowly pipe an elongated figure 8 about 2 to 3 inches long onto the sheet. Then, starting from the center of the figure, pipe 3 intersecting loops on the same side. Pipe designs or not, as you like, within each wing section. You should have enough chocolate to make plenty of extras in case of breakage. Freeze them for at least an hour before using. (They will keep in the freezer for 3 months.)

At serving time, garnish each mousse with a rosette of whipped cream and a butterfly or two.

From Chef Jim Dodge of the famed Fournou's Ovens in San Francisco.

Chocolate Mocha Roll

Serves 10–12
Preheat the oven to 375 degrees

Cake:

8 ounces semi-sweet chocolate
6 eggs, separated
⅛ teaspoon salt
¾ cup sugar
2 tablespoons unsweetened cocoa

Whipped cream filling:

2 tablespoons instant espresso
    coffee powder
2 tablespoons boiling water
2 cups heavy cream
½ cup confectioners' sugar

Buttercream icing:

4 egg whites
1¾ cups confectioners' sugar
½ pound butter, cut into 1-inch pieces,
    at room temperature
2 tablespoons instant espresso
    coffee powder
2 tablespoons boiling water

To make the cake, melt the chocolate in the top of a double boiler over hot water. Stir it until smooth, then remove from the heat. Beat the egg yolks in a bowl until they are well mixed; then slowly beat in the melted chocolate.

Beat the egg whites with the salt until soft peaks form. Beat in the sugar gradually until the whites are stiff and shiny, about 4 to 5 minutes. Fold the whites into the egg yolk-chocolate mixture.

Butter a jelly-roll pan and line it with wax or parchment paper. Butter the paper as well. Pour the batter into the pan and bake for 14 to 16 minutes, just until done. Do not let it become crisp and dry.

Remove the cake from the oven. Soak a layer of paper towels with water; wring them dry and immediately place them on top of the cake. Cover the wet towels with a layer of dry ones and let the cake rest this way for 20 minutes.

Carefully peel off the paper towels. Dust the cake with the cocoa and cover it with a dampened tea towel. Pull the corners tight and invert the pan. Remove the parchment or wax paper.

To make the filling, dissolve the coffee in the water and let it cool while you whip the cream, gradually adding the confectioners' sugar, until it is stiff. Stir in the cooled coffee and spread the cream over the cake. Roll the cake, jelly-roll fashion, place it on a serving plate or board, and refrigerate.

To make the icing, beat the egg whites with the confectioners' sugar in a medium-sized saucepan. Stir over low heat until the mixture is smooth and tepid. Transfer it to the bowl of an electric mixer and beat on medium speed for 20 minutes.

Gradually add the butter to the egg-white mixture and continue to beat until the mixture gathers onto the beaters, about 10 minutes. Dissolve the coffee in the boiling water and add to the mixture. Beat long enough to incorporate the coffee.

Spread the buttercream on the chilled cake roll and refrigerate the cake until ready to serve.

A genuine classic, Chocolate Mocha Roll was probably introduced to America by Dione Lucas, when she was teaching and running The Egg Basket restaurant in New York, some 25 years ago. Eileen Weinberg, Carolina's co-owner, used to own a very successful takeout food shop, Word of Mouth; pass the word that her variation on this famous collapsed soufflé (seen in the center front of a tableful of Carolina's chocolate specialties, above right) will make every true chocolate lover dissolve into blissful smiles.

Arizona Pecan Chocolate Rum Pie

Serves 6–8

¼ teaspoon salt
1¼ cups flour
½ cup lard, chilled
3 eggs, lightly beaten
3 tablespoons water
¼ teaspoon vinegar
1½ ounces unsweetened chocolate
3 tablespoons butter
¾ cup dark corn syrup
½ cup brown sugar
¾ teaspoon vanilla extract
1 tablespoon rum
1¼ cups chopped pecans

Mix the salt into the flour and cut in the lard. Measure out 1 tablespoon of the beaten eggs into a small bowl and reserve the remaining eggs. Add the water and vinegar to the bowl and stir. Slowly add the liquid to the flour and lard, just until the mixture holds together to form a dough.

Lightly flour a work surface and rolling pin and roll the dough into an 11-inch circle. Fit it into a 9-inch pie pan and refrigerate it if you plan to finish the pie after several hours, or freeze it if you are completing the recipe at this point. This will prevent shrinkage.

Melt the chocolate and butter together in a heavy saucepan. Set aside and allow to cool.

Stir the corn syrup and sugar into the reserved eggs. Add the chocolate and butter, vanilla, rum and the pecans. Mix well and pour into the pie shell.

Bake in the preheated oven for 1 hour, or until set. The filling will rise and then fall. Remove from the oven and cool on a rack. Serve slightly warm or at room temperature.

Arizona can be proud of this excellent pie, which may have its roots in Acadia. (The use of vinegar in the crust is the tipoff.) One of the offerings at Jerome's in Tucson, it is particularly popular with the lively crowd the restaurant regularly attracts.

Strange Drinks and Mocktails

it, whimsy and imagination dispatched scouts from the Bistro menu to the bar, and the signals coming back said, the beachhead is secure—send in the main force. Once again, Bistro patrons have led the charge in routing boredom!

The influence of the American Bistro on dining habits—indeed, dining philosophy—is that of a stone thrown into a placid lake. The ripples have spread out and touched other shores.

One shore that will never be the same again is the bar. Young Bistro clients are transforming the cocktail universe, as if riding Halley's comet and tucking under its tail all the tired anthologies of drinks inherited from the past.

No genuflecting to tradition for these adventurous spirits. Their choices are original: Curacao potions infused with a blue to make the ocean envious; Pertsovka Russian pepper vodka; peppermint and peach schnapps; the finest rums from the lazy Caribbean; inventive drinks sans alcohol. The martini, a survivor, retains its authority, but is more likely to be seen impertinently sporting a spear of pickled okra instead of the classic olive or lemon twist. Large sweet drinks are in, and Mexican is hot. Jalapeño peppers, floating like mines in a sea of gin, put the palate at risk. Soon, your favorite bistro may serve a margarita adorned with a coil of spaghetti and called a Conquistador Carbonara.

There is no special "place" for such novelties. With the help of Fedora, Kansas City may shake its beefy reputation. Fedora offers Bergamot de Czar, a mixture of high-voltage Smirnoff and Swiss pear soda. In Milwaukee, John Byron's delivers Gewürtztraminer juice straight up with a twist of lemon. New York City's America favors Russian Quaaludes (Canadian Club, Bailey's Irish Cream and Kahlua), while in San Francisco, the Balboa Café's version substitutes Stolichnaya for the whisky and adds Frangelico and cream, offering by way of palliative a

Fuzzy Navel (orange juice with 100-proof schnapps in a Pilsner glass).

And in Tucson, where the city fathers wisely forbid construction that would hide its intoxicating sky, Jerome's packages the Hurricane Cooler—light and dark rums, Pernod, orange, lemon and lime juices and a pineapple garnish, all doing a dervish dance in a giant tulip hurricane glass.

This spirit of jest is an extension of the new commandment that dining is theater and everyone gets into the act. Chefs now are missionaries in an unmapped land where the ability to entertain is as valuable as mastery of the saucepan, the oven or the skillet. The waitpersons hone their histrionic skills by declaiming the day's specials and adding ever more fantastical names to the menu.

Then there is the barkeep, the wizard who produces this wondrous array of potions with a coloratura flourish. Find such a magician and you will know you have struck gold, as in the departed days when you could only enter the classiest joints if you wore the "right" threads or rapped the correct tattoo on the speakeasy door.

A new dining and drinking world awaits, and you are Columbus, Pizarro, De Soto in quest of treasures. You will find them in the American Bistro. All you need is the uninhibited, playful spirit that has breached frontiers since Adam and Eve broke out of Eden.

Adventurous diners demand novelty and play from the bar, and are met with an array of strange drinks, whose garnishes range from glass animals, paper beachballs and glow-in-the-dark swizzle sticks to consumable items such as pickled okra, muddled strawberries and star-shaped ice cubes. In New York, above, staff at Memphis bid you welcome; at left, a couple at the Museum Café say Goodnight.

...And a Glass of Wine

ffered by the glass or uncorked at your table, a fine wine surrenders its pleasures by adding to yours.

As we all know, in the world of public and private romance, a touch of the grape is the magical ingredient that can pin wings to a plodding affair and launch it soaring toward the sun.

The evidence is there, taking an accountant's perspective, in the bitter commercial warfare being waged over the purse and palate of the American wine-drinking public. We, the joyful patrons of the American bistro, are the world's prime wine market. And the battle lines are drawn between the vintners of Europe and the upstart Yankees, whether their speech is accented by New York nasal, Ohio flat or California slide. It is like Saturday-morning wrestling on television—somewhat overdone, but an exhilarating spectator sport. The rest, you might say, is gravy—with a modest alcoholic content.

Without question, it was our choice of wine as the preferred social lubricant that set the stage for the evolution of the American bistro. The wine industry in this country has grown phenomenally in the last decade (wine grapes are now grown in 40 of our 50 states, and wines from them are marketed commercially).

Good wine brings good food along with it, and the blood line runs directly from wine bar to bistro. Wine-drinking is like grazing, one taste here, another there, the way we move from bistro to bistro in quest of new dining experiences.

Wine surrenders its pleasures by the sip, by the sniff. It is a companion, never a conquest. And above all, it invites variety. It is not a variety easy to attain, because the pasture yields few choices when you are grazing at a bar—mainly undistinguished house wines offered by the glass only.

That is all changing with the appearance of a dynamite piece of high-tech called the Cruvinet (originally imported from France, hence its name, but now being manufactured in America). The Cruvinet allows even the highest-quality wines to be served by the glass without deteriorating as a result of exposure to the air. It is an ingenious device—and also eye-catching, with polished spigots and glistening wood—that injects nitrogen into the bottle as it dispenses the wine. Nitrogen, an inert gas, seals the wine against damage, and the opened bottle can be kept for weeks.

Just imagine, a 1974 California Cabernet by the glass! Now you can duplicate the experience of wine-tasting professionals, flitting like a butterfly among the most exquisite nectars the good earth offers to the human palate. Cheers!

California Cafe
Bar & Grill

CABERNET SAUVIGNON
CALIFORNIA

CELLARED AND BOTTLED BY ROUND HILL VINEYARDS
ST. HELENA, CALIFORNIA • ALCOHOL 12.7% BY VOLUME

Above, a designer "house label" honors a fine wine's power to create an atmosphere that is both intimate and convivial, or to make a special occasion sublimely memorable. At left, New York's American Festival Café is glimpsed through the glass-bottled wall of its cellar of American wines. Next page: It's the end of a long evening and Mick's in Atlanta is empty—until tomorrow.

Appendix of Recipes

NOTE: *The recipes have been tested using large or extra-large eggs; unsalted sweet butter; all-purpose unbleached flour; and fresh heavy cream, not the ultra-pasteurized variety.*

Chicken Stock

Makes 4 quarts

7–8 pounds chicken parts
2 onions, peeled
2 stalks celery, sliced
1 leek, trimmed
1 carrot, sliced

Place all of the ingredients in a stock pot and cover them with cold water. Bring to a gentle boil, skim and reduce the heat. Simmer, partially covered, for 4 to 6 hours, skimming occasionally.

Pour the broth through a strainer lined with cheesecloth and refrigerate until the fat rises to the surface, and can be easily removed.

Turkey Stock

Makes 2 cups

Bones from a 10-to-15-pound turkey or turkey breast
2 leeks
1 onion
2 carrots
1½ gallons water

Place all the ingredients in a large pot. Bring to a boil, reduce the heat and simmer, skimming occasionally, until the liquid is reduced by half. This will take about 2 hours. Strain the stock into another pot and simmer until it is reduced to 2 cups.

VARIATION: Poultry Stock is made by using whatever bird bones you have available—pigeon, squab, quail, chicken, turkey, Cornish game hen, duck or pheasant—in place of a single kind of poultry.

Duck Stock

Makes 4–6 cups
Preheat the oven to 375 degrees

3 duck carcasses, wings and necks, chopped
2 carrots, cut into pieces
2 onions, cut into pieces
2 stalks celery, cut into pieces
6 black peppercorns
1 small bay leaf
2½ quarts water
Salt

Place the duck bones, wings, necks, and the vegetables in a heavy roasting pan and roast them, turning occasionally, until brown, about 1 hour.

Scrape the contents of the roasting pan into a 6- to 8-quart pot. Deglaze the roasting pan with water, if needed, and add to the pot. Add the peppercorns and bay leaf and water to the pot. Add more water, if needed, to cover the ingredients.

Bring the water to a fast simmer, skimming any foam that rises to the surface, for about 15 minutes. Reduce the heat and simmer, partially covered, for 2 to 3 hours.

Strain the liquid and return it to the pot. Discard the solids. Cook over high heat until the liquid is reduced to about 7 cups. Let it cool and add salt to taste.

Refrigerate overnight, or until all the fat rises to the top. Remove the fat. You can keep the stock, refrigerated, for 3 days, or freeze it for longer storage.

Mustard Thyme Butter

Makes about 2 tablespoons

1 tablespoon butter, softened
1 teaspoon finely chopped fresh thyme
1½ teaspoons Dijon mustard
⅛ teaspoon coarse salt
½ teaspoon fresh lemon juice
Freshly ground pepper

Combine all of the ingredients, stirring until smooth. Cover and refrigerate. Serve at room temperature.

Beurre Blanc

Beurre Blanc is a deservedly popular sauce in American bistros. In many of the recipes which use it, we have referred you to this page, but you may find that the ingredients listed will differ, because the different chefs want to flavor the reduction in original ways. Here is the method and the basic ingredients to use if others are not suggested.

Makes about 1 cup

1½ cups dry white wine
2 tablespoons champagne vinegar or fresh lemon juice
3 tablespoons finely chopped shallots
½ pound chilled, unsalted butter, cut into 24 pieces
Salt and freshly ground white pepper

Combine the wine, vinegar or lemon juice and the shallots in a heavy non-corrodible saucepan and cook over moderate heat until the liquid is reduced to about 2 tablespoons. This will take 15 to 20 minutes and the liquid will be syrupy. You can strain out the shallots, if you want a perfectly smooth sauce.

Remove the pan from the heat, to cool slightly, and then return it to low heat and whisk a few pieces of butter into the reduction, until the mixture looks creamy. Then beat in the remaining butter, piece by piece, whisking each addition until it disappears into the sauce, before adding more.

If the sauce begins to look oily around the edges, the heat is too high and the sauce will break. To save it, remove the pan from the heat and hold it in cold water for a minute or so, whisking until it regains consistency.

The finished sauce will be barely warm and have the soft, fluid consistency of barely whipped cream, but not be so thick that whisk marks are visible. Season it to taste with salt and white pepper.

Pesto

Makes 1 cup

2 cups packed fresh basil leaves
2 cloves garlic, sliced
2 tablespoons pine nuts
½ cup freshly grated parmesan cheese
½ cup extra-virgin olive oil

Place the basil, garlic, pine nuts and cheese in a food processor. Pulse a few times to chop the leaves. With the motor running, slowly pour in the olive oil.

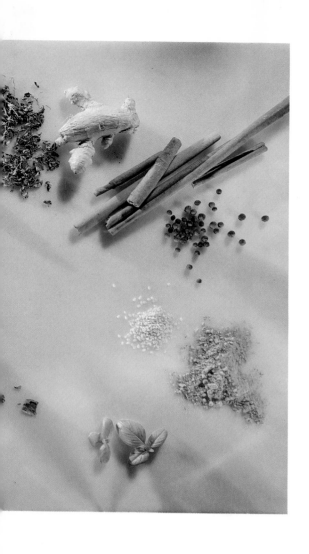

Roasting and Peeling Peppers

Preheat the broiler

Cut the peppers in half lengthwise and remove the ribs and seeds. Rinse them well and drain, then pat them dry. Place them, cut sides down, on a broiler pan and slide under the broiler. Adjust the broiler rack so that the pan is not so close to the heat that the peppers darken too quickly.

The object is to cook the peppers long enough for them to become tender, remain firm and blister, all at the same time. (If they have blackened too rapidly, pop the pan into a 400-degree oven for a few minutes.) Press down on the pepper halves with a folded kitchen towel, after they have cooked for about 5 minutes, so that they will blister more evenly.

When they are done, after about 8 to 10 minutes, transfer them to a brown paper bag and close the top, or cover them with a very damp towel for 15 minutes. This steam will help the skin peel more easily.

When the peppers are cool enough to handle, peel off the blackened skin with your fingers and a paring knife.

Toasting and Peeling Hazelnuts

Preheat the oven to 350 degrees

Place the hazelnuts in a baking pan and roast them for about 12 minutes, shaking the pan once or twice, until the nuts are golden beneath the skins. Wrap them in a clean dish towel and let them cool for 20 minutes. Remove their skins by rubbing them through the towel with your hands.

Your Own Cooks' Tour: More Than 100 Restaurants Well Worth Visiting

Country Inn at Princeton
30 Mountain Road
Princeton, MA 01541
617 464 2030

Restaurant Jasper
240 Commercial Street
Boston, MA 02109
617 523 1126

Seasons
The Bostonian Hotel
Faneuil Hall Marketplace
Boston, MA 02109
617 523 3600

Rarities
The Charles Hotel
1 Bennett Street
Cambridge, MA 02138
617 864 1200

Freshfields: A Country Bistro
Route 128
West Cornwall, CT 06796
203 672 6601

The Ballroom
253 West 28th Street
New York, NY 10001
212 244 3005

Gotham Bar & Grill
12 East 12th Street
New York, NY 10003
212 620 4020

Pizzapiazza
785 Broadway
New York, NY 10003
212 505 0977

Lola
30 West 22nd Street
New York, NY 10010
212 675 6700

Fifth Avenue Grill
102 Fifth Avenue
New York, NY 10011
212 741 3742

Quatorze
240 West 14th Street
New York, NY 10011
212 206 7006

Rogers & Barbero
149 Eighth Avenue
New York, NY 10011
212 243 2020

Texarkana Restaurant
64 West 10th Street
New York, NY 10011
212 254 5800

Exile
323 Greenwich Street
New York, NY 10013
212 219 8072

Manhattan Chili Company
302 Bleecker Street
New York, NY 10014
212 206 7163

Aurora
60 East 49th Street
New York, NY 10017
212 692 9292

Lavin's Restaurant
23 West 39th Street
New York, NY 10018
212 921 1288

American Festival Café
20 West 50th Street
New York, NY 10020
212 246 6699

An American Place
969 Lexington Avenue
New York, NY 10021
212 517 7660

Arcadia
21 East 62nd Street
New York, NY 10021
212 223 2900

JAMS
154 East 79th Street
New York, NY 10021
212 772 6800

Maxwell's Plum
1181 First Avenue
New York, NY 10021
212 628 2100

Safari Grill
1115 Third Avenue
New York, NY 10021
212 371 9090

Casual Quilted Giraffe
15 East 55th Street
New York, NY 10022
212 593 1221

The Four Seasons
99 East 52nd Street
New York, NY 10022
212 754 9494

Cafe des Artistes
1 West 67th Street
New York, NY 10023
212 877 3500

Metropolis
444 Columbus Avenue
New York, NY 10024
212 769 4444

Sarabeth's Kitchen
423 Amsterdam Avenue
New York, NY 10024
212 496 6280

Carolina
355 West 46th Street
New York, NY 10036
212 245 0058

The American Harvest Restaurant
The Vista International
3 World Trade Center
New York, NY 10048
212 938 9100

The Coast Grill
Noyac Road
Southampton, NY 11968
516 283 2277

Depuy Canal House
High Falls, NY 12440
914 687 7700

American Bounty
Culinary Institute of America
Route 9 North
Hyde Park, NY 12538
914 452 9600

Apropos
211 South Broad Street
Philadelphia, PA 19107
215 546 4424

Under the Blue Moon
8042 Germantown Avenue
Philadelphia, PA 19118
215 247 1100

Café Nola
328 South Street
Philadelphia, PA 19147
215 627 2590

Frog
1524 Locust Street
Philadelphia, PA 19103
215 735 8882

The Garden Restaurant
1617 Spruce Street
Philadelphia, PA 19193
215 546 4455

The American Café
1211 Wisconsin Avenue N.W.
Washington, DC 20007
202 337 3600

Windows at USA Today Building
1000 Wilson Boulevard
Rosslyn, VA 22209
703 527 4430

The Inn at Little Washington
Main & Middle Streets
Washington, VA 22747
703 675 3800

The Trellis
Duke of Gloucester Street
Williamsburg, VA 23185
804 229 8610

Pawleys Island Inn
P.O. Box 567
Highway 17
Pawleys Island, SC 29585
803 237 9033

Mick's
557 Peachtree Street
Atlanta, GA 30308
404 875 6425

Elizabeth's on 37th
105 East 37th Street
Savannah, GA 31401
912 236 5547

Louie's Backyard
700 Waddell Avenue
Key West, FL 33040
305 294 1061

Café Max
2601 East Atlantic Boulevard
Pompano Beach, FL 33062
305 782 0606

Max's Place
2268 N.E. 123rd Street
North Miami, FL 33181
305 893 6888

Chancellor's at Vanderbilt Plaza
2100 West End Avenue
Nashville, TN 37203
615 320 1700

Skoby's Restaurant
1001 Konnarock Road
Kingsport, TN 37664
615 246 6532

Sixth Avenue
600 West Main Street
Louisville, KY 40402
502 587 6664

Dudley's Restaurant
380 South Mill Street
Lexington, KY 40508
606 252 1010

Tapawingo Restaurant
9502 Lake Street
Ellsworth, MI 49729
616 588 7971

John Byron's
777 East Michigan Street
Milwaukee, WI 53202
414 277 0660

Primavera
275 Market Street
Minneapolis, MN 55405
612 339 8000

Printer's Row Restaurant
550 South Dearborn Street
Chicago, IL 60605
312 461 0780

Gordon
500 North Clark Street
Chicago, IL 60610
312 467 9780

95th Restaurant
John Hancock Center
Chicago, IL 60611
312 280 5450

Stephanie's
1825 North Knoxville Avenue
Peoria, IL 61603
309 682 7300

Richard Perry Restaurant
3265 South Jefferson Avenue
St. Louis, MO 63118
314 771 4100

American Restaurant
Crown Center
Kansas City, MO 64108
816 471 8050

Fedora Café & Bar
210 West 47th Street
Kansas City, MO 64112
816 561 6565

Brigtsen's Restaurant
723 Dante Street
New Orleans, LA 70118
504 861 7610

Copeland's
4338 St. Charles Avenue
New Orleans, LA 70115
504 897 2325

Commander's Palace
1403 Washington Avenue
New Orleans, LA 70130
504 899 8231

K-Paul's Louisiana Kitchen
416 Chartres Street
New Orleans, LA 70130
504 522 3818

Mr. B's
201 Royal Street
New Orleans, LA 70130
504 523 2078

Patout's
1846 Center Street
New Iberia, LA 70560
318 365 5206

Routh Street Café
3005 Routh Street
Dallas, TX 75201
214 871 7161

Mansion on Turtle Creek
2821 Turtle Creek Boulevard
Dallas, TX 75219
214 526 2121

Charley's 517
517 Louisiana
Houston, TX 77002
713 224 4438

Magnolia Bar & Grill
6000 Richmond Avenue
Houston, TX 77057
713 781 6207

Green Beanery Café
2121 McFaddin
Beaumont, TX 77701
409 833 5913

The Rattlesnake Club
901 Larimer
Denver, CO 80204
303 573 8900

Steven Restaurant
4333 North Brown Avenue
Scottsdale, AZ 85251
602 941 4936

Jerome's
6958 East Tanque Verde Road
Tucson, AZ 85715
602 721 0311

Massee's at the Winery
Galisteo and Water
Santa Fe, NM 87501
505 988 2984

The Garfield Grill
322 Garfield
Santa Fe, NM 87501
505 988 9562

Angeli Caffé/Pizzeria
7274 Melrose Avenue
Los Angeles, CA 90046
213 936 9086

Chaya Brasserie
8741 Alden Drive
Los Angeles, CA 90048
213 859 8833

Primi un Ristorante
10543 West Pico Boulevard
West Los Angeles, CA 90064
213 475 9235

Spago
1114 Horn Avenue
Los Angeles, CA 90069
213 652 4025

Trumps Restaurant
8764 Melrose Avenue
Los Angeles, CA 90069
213 855 1480

La Scala
9455 Santa Monica Boulevard
Beverly Hills, CA 90210
213 275 0579

Michael's
1147 Third Street
Santa Monica, CA 90403
213 451 0843

Hayes Street Grill
320 Hayes Street
San Francisco, CA 94102
415 863 5545

Stars
150 Redwood
San Francisco, CA 94102
415 861 7827

Bentley's
185 Sutter Street
San Francisco, CA 94104
415 898 6895

Campton Place
340 Stockton Street
San Francisco, CA 94108
415 781 5555

Fournou's Ovens
The Stanford Court Hotel
San Francisco, CA 94108
415 989 1910

Fog City Diner
1300 Battery Street
San Francisco, CA 94111
415 982 2000

Square One
190 Pacific at Front
San Francisco, CA 94111
415 788 1110

Café Americain
317 Columbus Avenue
San Francisco, CA 94133
415 981 8266

Mustards Grill
7399 St. Helena Highway
Napa, CA 94558
707 944 2424

Chez Panisse
1517 Shattuck Avenue
Berkeley, CA 94709
415 548 5049

Fourth Street Grill
1820 Fourth Street
Berkeley, CA 94705
415 849 0526

California Café
60 Belvedere Drive
Mill Valley, CA 94941
415 381 2611

New Boonville Hotel & Restaurant
Highway 128
Boonville, CA 94515
707 895 3478

Café Beaujolais
961 Ukiah Street
Mendocino, CA 95460
707 937 5614

Atwater's Restaurant
111 S.W. Fifth Avenue
Portland, OR 97204
503 220 3600

Fullers at the Seattle Sheraton
1400 Sixth Avenue
Seattle, WA 98101
206 621 9000

Rosellini's Other Place
319 Union Street
Seattle, WA 98101
206 623 7340

The Captain Whidbey Inn
2072 W. Whidbey Island Inn Road
Coupeville, WA 98239
206 678 4097

The Ark
Nahcotta, WA 98637
206 665 4133

Recipe Contributors

THE MELTING POT:
26-7 Tortilla, Pulpo and Eggplant from Felipe Rojas-Lombardi, The Ballroom, New York, NY. 28-9 Fritters and Eggplant Sandwiches from Lola, New York, NY. 30-1 Terrine by Anne Disrude, *Food & Wine*, September 1985; Pâté from Laura Thorne, The Coast Grill, Southampton, NY. 32-3 Cheesecake from Richard Perry, The Richard Perry Restaurant, St. Louis, MO; Mousse from Stephen Lyle, Quatorze, New York, NY. 34-5 Smoked Swordfish and Smoked Swordfish Salad from Phyllis Gosfield, Under the Blue Moon, Philadelphia, PA. 36-7 Cured Salmon, Bentley's, San Francisco, CA; Smoked Goose from Kenneth Dunn, American Restaurant, Kansas City, MO. 39 Chicken from Lavin's, New York, NY; Steak from Cindy Pawlcyn, Mustards Grill, Napa, CA. 40-1 Shrimp from John Schenk, Fifth Avenue Grill, New York, NY; Squab from Jeremiah Tower, Stars, San Francisco, CA; from *Jeremiah Tower's New American Cooking*, Harper & Row, 1986. 43 Peppers from Marcel Desaulniers, The Trellis, Williamsburg, VA; Pizzelle from John Pawula, Stephanie's, Peoria, IL. 44-5 Blini from Louis Osteen, Pawleys Island Inn, Pawleys Island, SC; Corn Pancakes from Bruce J. Auden, Charley's 517, Houston, TX; Cornmeal Pancakes from Larry Forgione, An American Place, New York, NY. 46-7 Spinach Pizza from PizzaPiazza, New York, NY; Prosciutto Pizza from Wolfgang Puck, Spago Restaurant, Los Angeles, CA, as it appeared in *Chocolatier*, January 1984. 48 Fettuccine from Harlan Peterson, Tapawingo, Ellsworth, MI. 50-1 Buckwheat Pasta from Anne Rosenzweig, Arcadia, New York, NY; Calzone from LaScala Presto Trattoria, Beverly Hills, CA. 53 Ragout from Jimmy Schmidt, Rattlesnake Club, Denver, CO. 54 Duck from Larry Forgione, An American Place, New York, NY. 56 Chili from Michael McLaughlin, Manhattan Chili Parlor, New York, NY; Jambalaya from Emeril Lagasse, The Commander's Palace, New Orleans, LA. 58-9 Chicken from Bruce J. Auden, Charley's 517, Houston, TX; Pork from Norman van Aken, Louie's Backyard, Key West, FL. 60-1 Lobster from Mark Militello, Café Max, Pompano Beach, FL; Sausage from Michael Roberts, Trumps, Los Angeles, CA. 64-5 Soup from Mark Peel, Maxwell's Plum, New York, NY; Lobster from Walter Zuromski, Rarities, Cambridge, MA. 66-7 Chanterelle from Lorren Garlichs, Captain Whidbey Inn, Coupeville, WA; Shiitake from Patrick O'Connell, Inn at Little Washington, Little Washington, VA, as seen in *The New York Times*, July 24, 1985. 68-9 Apples from Larry Forgione, An American Place, New York, NY; Veal from Billy Della Ventura, 95th Restaurant, Chicago, IL.

CORNUCOPIA:
72-3 Squab from Stephen Lyle, Quatorze, New York, NY; Rabbit from Steve Mangan, Freshfields, West Cornwall, CT. 74-5 Duckling Salad from Jasper White, Restaurant Jasper, Boston, MA; Baked Duck from Lorren Garlichs, Captain Whidbey Inn, Coupeville, WA. 76-7 Quail from John Pawula, Stephanie's, Peoria, IL; Pheasant from Steve Mangan, Freshfields, West Cornwall, CT. 78-9 Quail from Dean Fearing, The Mansion at Turtle Creek, Dallas, TX; Rabbit from John Pawula, Stephanie's, Peoria, IL. 81 Turkey from Kathy Pavletich Casey, Fullers, Seattle, WA. 82-3 Wild Turkey from Bradley Ogden, Campton Place, San Francisco, CA, as it appeared in *Chocolatier*, Winter, 1984; Pigeon from Michael McCarty, Michael's, Santa Monica, CA.

FOODS FROM THE WATERS:
86-7 Cassoulet from Michael Foley, Printer's Row, Chicago, IL; Bluefish from Fedora, Kansas City, MO. 88-9 Shrimp from Kenneth Dunn, American Restaurant, Kansas City, MO; Monkfish from Marcel Desaulniers, The Trellis, Williamsburg, VA. 90-1 Trout from Lavin's, New York, NY; Sole from Billy Della Ventura, 95th Restaurant, Chicago, IL. 92-3 Bass from Piero Selvaggio, Primi un Ristorante, Los Angeles, CA; Halibut from Kathy Pavletich Casey, Fullers, Seattle, WA. 94-5 Tuna from Primavera, Minneapolis, MN; Oysters from Bentley's, San Francisco, CA. 96-7 Tuna from Exile, New York, NY; Scallops from Michael McCarty, Michael's, Santa Monica, CA. 98-99 Snapper from The Garden, Philadelphia, PA. 100-1 Halibut from Walter Zuromski, Rarities, Cambridge, MA; Shrimp from Elizabeth Terry, Elizabeth's at 37th Street, Savannah, GA. 102-3 Caviar from Mark Militello, Café Max, Pompano Beach, FL; Salmon from Café Beaujolais, Mendocino, CA.

DOWN HOME COOKING:
106-7 Oyster Loaf from Jimella Lucas, The Ark, Nahcotta, WA; Chicken from Billy Della Ventura, 95th Restaurant, Chicago, IL. 108-9 French Toast from François Keller, American Festival Café, New York, NY; Corn Pudding from Walter Plendner, American Harvest, New York, NY. 110-1 Beignets from Mr. B's, New Orleans, LA; Shad Roe from François Keller, American Festival Café, New York, NY. 113 Monterey Jack from Seppi Renggli, The Four Seasons, New York, NY; Pork from Evan Kleiman, Angeli, Los Angeles, CA, as it appeared in *Cucina Fresca* by E. Kleiman and V. LaPlace, Harper & Row, 1985. 114-5 Cheese Biscuits from Elizabeth Terry, Elizabeth's at 37th Street, Savannah, GA; Biscuits from Billy Della Ventura, 95th Restaurant, Chicago, IL; Dill Rolls from Jim Heywood, American Bounty, Hyde Park, NY, as seen in *Great American Cooking*, Woman's Day SuperSpecial, April 1984. 118-9 Bran Muffins from Nanci Main, The Ark, Nahcotta, WA; Dumplings from Steve Mangan, Freshfields, West Cornwall, CT. 120-1 Soufflé from Emeril Lagasse, The Commander's Palace, New Orleans, LA; Pudding from Jim Dodge, Fournou's Ovens, San Francisco, CA. 122-3 Shortcake from Walter Plendner, American Harvest, New York, NY; Pudding from Bruce J. Auden, Charley's 517, Houston, TX. 124 Grunt from Richard Perry, The Richard Perry Restaurant, St. Louis, MO.

ANYTHING GOES (IN THE KITCHEN)!
128-9 Tortilla from Dean Fearing, The Mansion at Turtle Creek, Dallas, TX; Pumpkin from Bill Geary, Atwater's, Portland, OR. 130-1 Watercress from Margaret Fox, Café Beaujolais, Mendocino, CA; Red Pepper from Joyce Goldstein, Square One, San Francisco, CA. 132-3 Cream of Leek from Sanford D'Amato, John Byron's, Milwaukee, WI; Black Bean from Michael Roberts, Trumps, Los Angeles, CA. 134-5 Autumn Salad from John Schenk, Fifth Avenue Grill, New York, NY; Pepper Salad from Leslie Revsin, Metropolis, New York, NY. 136-7 Potato Salad from Albert Portale, Gotham Bar & Grill, New York, NY; Greens Salad from Kathy Pavletich Casey, Fullers, Seattle, WA. 138-9 Lentil Salad from Mick's, Atlanta, GA; Fruit Salad from Seppi Renggli, The Four Seasons, New York, NY as seen in *Food & Wine*, June 1985. 140 Salmon Salad from Albert Portale, Gotham Bar & Grill, New York, NY; Greens Salad from Kenneth Dunn, American Restaurant, Kansas City, MO. 142-3 Rapini from Evan Kleiman, Angeli, Los Angeles, CA; Artichokes from Christian Iser, Fournou's Ovens, San Francisco, CA. 144-5 Escarole from Daniel Malzhan, Café Americain, San Francisco, CA; Salmon from Tim Ryan, American Bounty, Hyde Park, NY, as seen in *Food & Wine*, June 1985. 146-7 Sausage from Albert Portale, Gotham Bar & Grill, New York, NY; Tortelloni from Fedora, Kansas City, MO. 148-9 Mousse, Tuiles and Puree from Anne Rosenzweig, Arcadia, New York, NY; Ice Cream from Lindsey Remolif Shere, Chez Panisse, Berkeley, CA; from her book *Chez Panisse Desserts*, Random House 1985. 150-1 Turtle Cay Bananas from Jeremiah Tower, Stars, San Francisco; from *Jeremiah Tower's New American Cooking*, Harper & Row 1986; Ice from Bruce J. Auden, Charley's 517, Houston, TX; Tarts from Sanford D'Amato, John Byron's, Milwaukee, WI. 152-3 Pancakes with Cider Ice Cream from Nancy Silverton, Maxwell's Plum, New York, NY; from *Desserts by Nancy Silverton*, Harper & Row 1986. 154-5 Cheesecake from Leslie Mackie, Restaurant Jasper, Boston, MA; Pudding from Barry Wine, The Casual Quilted Giraffe, New York, NY. 156-7 Cake from Stephan Pyles, Routh Street Café, Dallas, TX; Mousse from Jim Dodge, Fournou's Ovens, San Francisco, CA. 158-9 Roll from Carolina, New York, NY, as it appeared in *Chocolatier*, Summer, 1984; Pie from Jerome's, Tucson, AZ.

Photograph Credits

We would like to express particular appreciation to the following photographers: Ted Hardin, Peter Johansky, Nancy McFarland, Irene Stern, David Wasserman, Bruce Wolf. The following abbreviations are used in crediting their photographs: TH Ted Hardin; PJ Peter Johansky; NM Nancy McFarland; IS Irene Stern; DW David Wasserman; BW Bruce Wolf.

3 TH 5 PJ 7 Lon Cooper—Courtesy of Anne Rosenzweig 9 Mick Hales 10 Both: DW 11 top DW; bottom NM 12 DW 14 top BW; bottom DW 15 BW 16 Michael Darly 17 top DW; bottom BW 18-9 Jim D'Addio—Courtesy Grandesign 21 top DW; bottom left Courtesy American Harvest, right Courtesy Primavera 22-3 Jon Naar 24 top Courtesy The Ballroom; bottom Peter Poulides 25 TH 26 Harold Naideau 28-9 Mark Jenkinson 30-1 PJ 32 DW 33 TH 34 NM 35 Lester Sloan 36-7 W.H. Hodge—Peter Arnold, Inc. 37 Courtesy Café Americain 38 top Michael Geiger, bottom PJ 40 Dick Busher—Courtesy Atwater's 41 Fred Lyon 42 top BW; bottom George Robinson—F-Stop 44 Courtesy Pauleys Island 45 George Riley—F-Stop 46-7 Courtesy Spago 48 Courtesy Tapawingo 49 NM 50 PJ 50-1 Courtesy Pizzeria Uno 52 IS 55 top Ross Horowitz; bottom DW 57 top Ross Horowitz; bottom Fred Lyon 58 Terry Moore 59 Courtesy Louie's Backyard 60-1 Courtesy Copeland's 61 Terry Moore 62-3 Matthew Klein 64 Both: Brian Hagiwara 66 Courtesy Captain Whidbey's 67 DW 69 Matthew Klein 70-1 BW 72 TH 73 Courtesy Freshfields 74 TH 75 Courtesy Captain Whidbey's 76 Courtesy Stephanie's 76-7 IS 79 top Tom Brakefield—Tauras; bottom Peter Poulides 80 left Russell Abraham—Courtesy Shooting Stars; right Robert Milne—Courtesy Fullers 82 Terry Moore 83 left Fred Lyon; right Courtesy Michael's 84-5 top Terry Moore; bottom Ross Horowitz 85 top Don Gray—F-Stop; bottom Fred Lyon 86 NM 86-7 Courtesy 95th 87 IS 88 Susan Wood 89 NM 90-1 Both: IS 91 Courtesy Lavin's 92 Robert Milne—Courtesy Fullers 92-3 TH 94-5 Courtesy Bentley's 95 Courtesy Primavera 96 NM 97 Courtesy Louie's Backyard 98 top Edwin D. Dewees—Courtesy The Garden; bottom PJ 99 Matthew Klein 101 both: Peter Poulides 102 Rick Bolen 103 Brian Hagiwara 104 Jan Staller—Courtesy Grandesign 104-5 Courtesy Skobey's 105 Courtesy Pawleys Island 106 DW 107 Rick Bolen 108 NM 109 TH 110-1 IS 112-3 Both: Myron Beck—Courtesy Angeli 114-1 IS 115 Jim D'Addio—Courtesy Grandesign 116-7 Susan Wood 118 Lester Sloan 120 DW 121 Peter Poulides 122 Courtesy Dudley's 123 Courtesy The Ballroom 124-5 PJ 125 © 1982 Schroeder/Eastwood—Courtesy Inn at Little Washington 126 Courtesy Pawleys Island 127 top Courtesy The Trellis; bottom Courtesy John Byron's 128 Peter Poulides 129 R. Krubbner, Armstrong Roberts 130 Terry Moore 130-1 DW 131 Vincent Lee 132 Courtesy Trumps 133 Lester Sloan 134-5 IS 136-7 left Robert Milne; right Image First Photography—both Courtesy Fullers 138 DW 138-9 NM 139 David Michael Kennedy 141 top PJ; bottom Elizabeth Hathon 142 IS 142-3 Courtesy Stanford Court Hotel 143 W.H. Hodge—Peter Arnold Inc. 144-5 top Courtesy Café Americain; bottom David Michael Kennedy 146 BW 147 NM 148 Brian Hagiwara 149 BW 150-1 Vincent Lee 151 Courtesy Chaya 152 David Frazier 153 TH 154 David Frazier 155 top Michael Skott; bottom DW 157 Ross Horowitz 158 H. Gritscher—Peter Arnold Inc. 159 Ross Horowitz 160 Jan Staller—Courtesy Grandesign 161 TH 162-3 TH 163 Courtesy California Café 164-5 Courtesy Mick's 166-7 All: IS 168-9 NM 169 IS

Cover credit: Jan Staller—Courtesy Grandesign; architects and interior designers, Grandesign Architects PC

Index